D1737672

# EYE OF THE LEOPARD

# EYE OF THE LEOPARD

photography by **Beverly Joubert**

written by **Dereck Joubert**

foreword by **Lieutenant General Ian Khama**
President of the Republic of Botswana

RIZZOLI
NEW YORK

First published in the United States of America in 2009
by Rizzoli International Publications, Inc.
300 Park Avenue South, New York, NY 10010
www.rizzoliusa.com

2009 2010 2011 2012 / 10 9 8 7 6 5 4 3 2 1

ISBN-13: 978-0-8478-3322-1

Designed by Aldo Sampieri and Sarah Rachmann

Printed in China

Library of Congress Catalog Control Number: 2009922208

# FOREWORD

For years I missed seeing leopards. I'd be just a moment too late, or the vehicle following would see one. We'd sit for hours watching a patch of grass, convinced that it harbored a spotted cat, or drive endlessly in circles through the bush after an alarm call by impala. Then one day, at Mombo I saw a large male step out of the undergrowth and I understood why the Jouberts have been so fascinated by these cats for so long. One look into those amber eyes and you know that you are seeing a truly wild cat. And it's that wildness that so symbolizes the Okavango, Botswana, and wild Africa. It's something we have that no other continent has at this scale. Where else can you stand in one place and see dozens of species of animals, hundreds of birds, and thousands of hectares of pristine wild land? And somewhere out there, two filmmakers and National Geographic Explorers are busy going about their business, quietly, without a lot of fuss, without making a show of getting up close or interfering, prodding, or provoking animals, or turning them into curiosity items just there for our entertainment. That deep respect for those wild places, and those amber-eyed predators is what I have always seen from Dereck and Beverly, and in this unique and creative work it comes across quite plainly. It is no wonder that great awards and accolades follow them, from Emmy and Peabody Awards to the recent World Ecology Award, which puts them in the company of a handful of notables, like Richard Leakey, the Prince of Wales, the Aga Khan, and Jane Goodall. If you have seen the delights of our country on television, it is most likely through one of their films. I have been delighted and shocked by their stories.

But I know Dereck and Beverly best and most fondly from days sitting around a campfire outside, debating the future of lions or elephants and the crisis of the planet and talking about the lessons they have learned from the hours, months, and years they have spent getting closer to nature than just about anyone else in the world.

We all thank you.

Lieutenant General Seretse Khama Ian Khama
PRESIDENT OF THE REPUBLIC OF BOTSWANA

Opposite: *Striking poses is what leopards do best in areas where there is no threat from hunters. In those areas, they can melt away into invisibility in an instant.*

Following spread: *At the heart of Tortillis's range is a huge baobab tree, a landmark that must have been in her consciousness from the beginning, in her mother's range, and in fact stretching back over 5,000 generations of leopards in her bloodline. It is little wonder that she feels so comfortable in its embrace.*

# INTRODUCTION

We dedicate this book to the 12,000 leopards that have been shot quite legally in Africa since we started working on this book (between 2003 and 2009).

We have spent 28 years working in the wild in Africa, not a short time by any means, but for us, only just enough to scratch the surface of what we intended to find out. Our quest is to find the real Africa, that hidden soul of the wild part of this continent, because I believe the place where we live, or chose to, reflects who we are, our rhythms, patterns, passions. Our location changes us and in some way makes us different from before. And because this is the place where Man was born, it reflects who we once were and explains to some degree, where our instincts come from.

Big Cats have shared this space with us for at least 3.5 million years, so their pace is in many ways ours, and their fate shadows ours. They hunted us relentlessly for most of our history, and now we kill them indiscriminately. And yet, this love-hate relationship is so very important to us, not because we like to be hunted, but because something in us wants to be in touch with that ancient wildness inside. It keeps us guessing about some of our moods, reactions, and instincts. Knowing that these feelings are real anchors us, and gives us a place in the world. If nothing else distinguishes us, we are at least the ape that questions who we are.

Since we were born, leopards have declined from 700,000 to maybe 100,000, some say 50,000, and lions from nearly half a million to around 20,000. There have never been so few of these animals, and we have seen their demise as a direct result of our success, if reaching 6.7 billion people is a success.

It is a travesty, this modern-day enjoyment of killing and the causing of pain and suffering. Mankind is so good at times. We make beautiful things, we rally to rectify wrongs, join hands to help alleviate human suffering…and then pick up a gun and destroy something as clearly miraculous and beautiful as a cat like this. Sometimes it's so hard to see that goodness within us.

But it is there, and that is what keeps us going. Understanding the beat of these big cats is why we came to this place, because it allows us to know ourselves better.

*Explore the new worlds,*
*And you live a thousand lives.*
*Laugh, cry, nurse a wound,*
*Look into eyes of sorrow.*

*And when you return,*
*Having circled all the world,*
*The old faces and place,*
*Will be like exploring once again.*

Above: *Our world, our life, is made up of exploring, adventures, and living every second against one of the most dramatic backdrops in the world.*

Following spread: *Demure cats, these leopards, always tempting you with a glance, and flirting with your senses.*

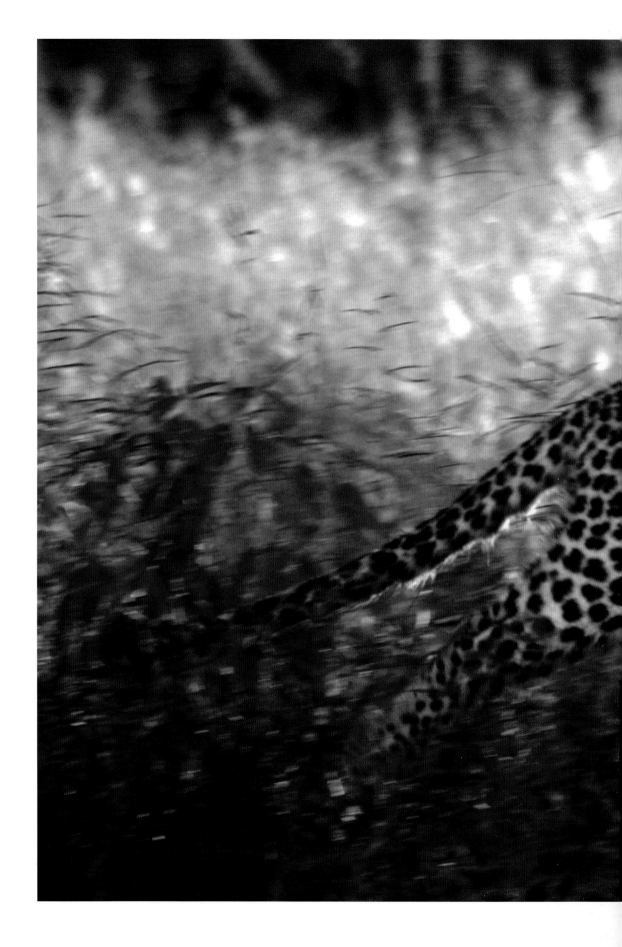

You are an ancient,
Dancer in the tall grasses.
Yes I will trust you,

Lead me to that place of peace,
That womb of warmth and sunlight,
That cave of paintings
Where we have danced before.

From a time long past

At the moment of action, the veil drops and the leopard is revealed.

A friend of ours here in Botswana tells the story with conviction that the progression of Man emerging from the group of apelike creatures, Australopithecines, and becoming "Homo" (habilis, erectus and finally Homo sapiens...the wise man) has now developed into two varieties, two divergent groups that may in time split. Our friend only recognizes one: Homo sapiens nobilis, the advanced, noble, wise ape. This group, unlike the other, is concerned about the environment, is educated on what the planet is undergoing under the weight of our use and waste, and is concerned enough to do the noble and right thing to correct that.

The other group forges on regardless, developing and using plastics, wasting, spewing chromium, carbon, and other chemicals out into the air, pumping toxic waste into rivers, hunting big cats, and doing business as if there was no tomorrow. In this, the second group may be right. There may be no tomorrow. Nobilis is at war with the second group, but the second group is at war with us all, and it will continue.

So I prefer to call the new breed Homo sapiens "compassionatus." This book is for those who align themselves with the more compassionate subgroup of hominids.

This book is not about the science of leopards, nor is it about the conservation of these cats. It is a celebration of an animal, just one of her kind, a young leopard who completely seduced us.

It is also a lament for what it will most likely be like in 15 or 20 years when they will have disappeared. When we started out, we believed that celebration and reverence was the answer to conservation. We filmed the big cats and other wildlife in Africa primarily to take their stories to the world, in the hope that perhaps the exposure would break down some of that misunderstanding that "the wild is out to get you," that predators lurk behind every tree, hunting you, creating some dangerous encounter, ready to instill some everlasting fear into your life.

So we camp, fly from location to location, film, cart our gear from one place to the next, sleep in the back of our vehicle, walk, track, get malaria, snake bites and scorpion stings, have many laughs and much craziness. And that is our life.

*Did we find her, or did she find us? I sometimes wonder.*

# ACT I

We all have an Act I, that moment when you know that this particular story or part of your life has begun.

Within a day of starting our project on leopards, we found a leopardess moving around a fallen tree. She moaned and snarled at us, so we stayed back. Then as she relaxed, there was a movement from inside the log. From the milky eyes and size, we placed the cub at eight days old.

Our project began right there, and the following four years of our lives would be dedicated to this, to these two cats, and to finding out all that we could about them. As it turns out, the cub led us back to that place we once knew, a place that we didn't know we had lost, an exciting world in the bush where everything was fresh and new.

You will know this cub as you view the first close-up images, in the same way we have for years, by a single stray whisker mark, a spot on the right lip. It is the one spot out of line in between the top and the second row, an undisciplined, mischievous spot that refused to conform, much like the character of this cat. It was there when we first found her, and it is there now, and like many things of beauty, it is this imperfection that is the beauty. Locating a single spot on a leopard may seem ridiculous, but when you know which spot to look for, it stands out 100 meters away.

We were following the cub one day, when she was already four months old. Suddenly the sky thickened and one of those fantastic African storms slammed down on us. The cub slipped away into a thicket. We decided to be real troupers and wait out the storm, afraid that any rushing around might scare the cub and make it shy more from our presence. Suddenly the area around us brightened and a bolt of lighting smashed a tree a few meters away, deafening both of us and showering us with leaves and debris. I looked around expecting to see the cub racing off, and possibly associating that noise with us, but instead, she was on the run, straight for us. She was terrified, and chose to snuggle up against the side of the vehicle, at my foot, where she sat until the storm had passed, looking out at the flashing skies and torturous lashes of rain.

Three good Batswana friends and guides at Mombo—Brookes, Celi, and Francis—listened to the story that night, huddled briefly, and then announced her name. It was to be "Legadema," which means Light from the Sky (or Lightning).

Legadema was christened, at last. It could have been an easier name, and in the two films in which she has featured, Jeremy Irons rolled the name around his Shakespearian-trained and Irish-born vocal cords more than once to get it right for the narration.

*Dawn is our favorite time to be with the leopards, and to catch that moment when they stretch the cold out of their bones and start the day.*

# PASSION

There is a great intensity in the wild heart. Nature rewards passion. Life rewards passion. People who understand this wildness in us, understand that in Africa no day can ever be called normal or mundane, or dispassionate, not when the explosive growl of leopards ruptures the blanket of bird and insect calls or a distant lion roar makes the hair on your arm stand up. There is always something to hang the moment of the day on, always something new. Being open to those things often seems to unlock them.

There had been mating within the general Mombo population of leopards a few months before we arrived. We didn't know this when we unpacked our gear and headed out with a map of the area that was drawn in my journal by a friend.

To fully describe the place we first saw as we drove out, you have to have an idea of your own personal paradise. Ours is Mombo, with its almost overwhelming numbers and variety of wildlife. It is the most prolific and varied wildlife experience I have come across anywhere in Africa so far. To say that animals are thick on the ground wouldn't be an exaggeration. But for me, Mombo is much more than that. Its forests of ebony trees pristinely tower above the other groves and outcrops of trees as shafts of light cut through leaves and cut hard edges onto the soft ground, creating a stage for dust particles to play in the air, dancing up and down the light ladders. The grunts of hippos bounce around the amphitheater of trees, distorting the sounds and making it appear as though the very forest itself is groaning under the effort of the day.

It is also a flash of crimson from a shrike darting across to the spiky protection of a low acacia, and the clucking of a family of warthogs as they run along as if their bellies are filled with pebbles from the river. But, of course, here the river doesn't have pebbles because Mombo is at the very tip of the biggest island in the Moremi Game Reserve deep in the heart of Botswana's Okavango Delta. Here there are no rocks, just the silty deposits of sand as the waters part around this arrow-like island. Mombo is that very tip, that arrowhead, a place that has the soul of Botswana in its grasp, exposed and re-grown millions of times as the floods come down each winter and then retreat again. It is the pioneering feel of Mombo that best calls to the deepest desire in Beverly and me to explore and forge new ideas, and step into the unknown.

As much as I respect science and the pursuit of knowledge, sometimes in our lives we have found that there is as much understanding in just being in a place or in the presence of an animal…for a long time, silently, moving slowly closer intellectually, step by step, without physically changing position.

It's what Beverly and I call "ghost" knowledge, because it has neither words, nor physical graphs or charts, but it floats just outside of our quantifying minds. Our brains hunger for facts and evidence, and yet so yearn for magic.

It is our passion.

*The relationship between Tortillis and Burnt Ebony, her mate, was always tense as they had to relearn each other, to understand what stage of their lives they were in. Once they mated, that relationship dissolved again into the void of coughs and rasping calls in the night.*

*By the miracle of nature, these solitary cats find each other in the wilderness of space and engage.*

Above: *A deadly dance of mating that is at one moment passionate and gentle, the next an explosion of fury and slashing claws and teeth reveals growls that rival the distant thunder in intensity.*

Opposite: *The pent up tension of mating can sometimes expose even a shy leopard for an instant more than usual.*

The flashing tango of leopards as they mate is as vital an ingredient of life here as filling your lungs through the filter of thick air in the forest, something that seems as though it wants to be taken for granted, but defies that possibility by its exceptional value. Some ancient religions have suggested that in that moment of passion we are closer to God than at any other time. Certainly we are closer to being unveiled, honest, our true selves, and as such, probably more instinctually transparent than at most other times. So it seems ironic that we are often thought of as being purest when we are most like animals, or perhaps most in touch with our animal selves.

It seems like nothing begins or ends without passion. Sometimes it is hard, brutal spitting passion or sad anxiety, but at other times that contorting seed of creativity grows inside of you.

For many it is the anxiety of a lover's look that may signal the first signs of distrust or boredom that could end this euphoria. Working with this leopard meant that some days we had the gnawing impressions of a dream that the leopard had been lost in the growls and cat fight sounds from the night, that we might never see her again, or that we might somehow fail in our task to understand what her existence was all about.

Sometimes it was the anxiety of the passion itself, in that we worried constantly that we would reveal too much, make her and her kind too commonplace, too understandable, too easy to kill. And most of all, perhaps it is walking that fine line between passion and obsession, or so I always thought.

On a misty day one February, I got out of the vehicle, head down, puzzling over some quite confusing tracks. It had rained. And while Beverly stood up high on the vehicle listening, I struck a line across the track with a stick to make sure that if I were to lose the direction and double back, I would know I had already seen this track. But there were two tracks and the marks on the ground confused me. Scuffs and turns, sand flicked to one side, and the deep impression of a shoulder. Was there a fight perhaps, an injured leopard? From the thicket nearby I heard a low growl rise in intensity and I knew that I was either in trouble, or there was some wild, passionate liaison happening nearby. In reality, at this distance it could have been both! If the male had seen me crouching down looking at tracks, I am sure he would have attacked, because I knew this male. It was a male from the burned ebony tree—Legadema's father—a cat with no fear of anything.

*It is a wild dance,*
*Swirling, swaying, moving like fire.*
*Angry, loving dance.*
*You stop and start, lead, follow.*

*Dance of the circle.*
*Is it death you seek?*
*Or life, passion, obsession!*
*It runs in your blood.*

These were the first courting leopards we had seen at Mombo, the first in nearly 20 years.

Following the tracks of mating leopards reminded me of a day when after a long run of sitting, doing very little but watching a leopard sleep its day away, we drove back to camp. A crimson blanket of clouds ribboned across at sunset from the horizon to above our heads and I took Beverly's hand and stepped out. We silently touched and swayed into the first steps of a tango. The hard, sun-baked sand was as good a dance floor as any, and the only sand that flicked was as Beverly did a guncha, one of those hair-raising (if you are the male recipient of such a move) kicks that narrowly misses (if one is lucky) all vital organs but flies up between one's legs. It's a tango step not to be attempted at home. We danced away our sadness and sore backs in a series of swirls and kicks, thankful to be alone and unobserved, owners for a moment of the whole world's quiet places and beautiful things.

The sun seemed to stay hovering a little longer, and the nearby zebras and wildebeest watched for a while and then put their heads down again. We have tangoed a lot in our lives. And it is passionate. So much so that I feel awkward dancing the tango with anyone besides Beverly.

So when I had my head down looking at the tracks, I should have understood what I was seeing and not been as surprised as I was when nearby the bushes erupted into growls and roars.

As we walked away on that sunset tango day, we looked back and Beverly said, "I wonder what a great Bushman tracker would make of all that?" The circles and scuffs on the hard ground looked like the most confusing combination of footprints you could imagine. I studied them like a passing Bushman or Shangaan might, as if I didn't know their origin. "He would look at this part, then over here, and probably make his pronouncement to the waiting clan…'Tango!'"

*The intensity of leopards is reflected in everything they do, each movement, every gesture.*

# LIFE

No education, no journey into life, is easy without a guide. The cub, Legadema, lay folded into the embrace of her mother, Tortillis, who was named after her liking of living in the high Acacia tortillas treetops near the Mombo Camp, the best place for viewing the world. She was a tree cat, living in and out of holes in sausage trees (Kigelia) and sometimes visiting a regular perch in an ancient baobab tree. As this 500-year-old tree softly embraced her, she looked as if she had draped herself there a thousand times over hundreds of years. Perhaps she had. Her line of female leopards must stretch back to the beginning of their time here.

She had mated, given birth, lost her cubs, and mated again five times without once nurturing a cub beyond three months. This was the sixth attempt at motherhood and we wondered how this could be sustainable. Each step of the way, we saw parallels. Of course, anything more productive than her present success rate would result in an explosion of leopards and problems not too dissimilar to what we are going through ourselves as we nudge up against 6.7 billion people and one small territory called Earth.

But she sniffed the front of the vehicle and looked at us for a long minute and then relaxed. She wanted to make very sure that her cub was going to be safe. She was the guardian and guide, and her time had at last come.

In our case, although unaware of it at this moment, we were meeting our own guardian and guide. One that would take us on a journey to places unknown.

In our previous work with lions, we had specialized in understanding, researching, and filming their hunting behavior. As a result we've logged thousands of observed kills. It has been a great opportunity for science. But it has also been a burden. Seeing wave after wave of newborn zebras cut down by lions and hyenas, and buffalo calves bowled over time and again, eventually wears you down. We've seen baby zebras taken by hyenas as they are being born, before their feet touch the ground, and hippos literally eaten in half before they succumb. In this business you learn to toughen up.

We weren't looking for anything else on this project but to work with a fresh species. What we found was the perfect guide to refresh our passion: Legadema.

From the first day we found her, she soaked up the world in a way that I have never been aware of any animal doing before. You can romanticize things easily when you are on the edge of the world, so I tend to lean the opposite way. After 30 years in the bush, sitting with lions and trying so hard to understand who they are and what is going on inside their minds, I was finally left with the cold, hard scientific fact that in reality they are largely about filling those hungry bellies. Looking into the eyes of this leopard showed hints of something different. We set ourselves a task: to try to determine what behavior she learned, and what she could not have acquired any other way but by some kind of hard wiring. To do that, we needed to spend as much time as possible with her, so that no lessons were being taught by Tortillis that we were not aware of. That meant we had to be with her as many hours a day as humanly possible.

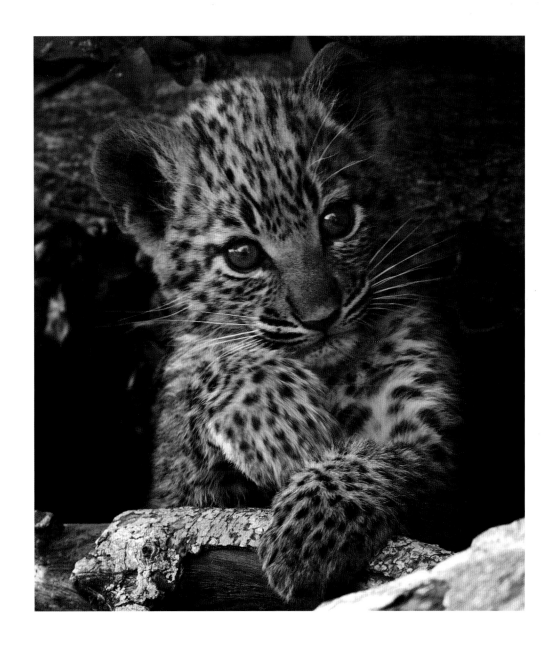

Above: *At just weeks old, their lives are so fragile and their dependence on their mothers so extreme that most cubs die within a month.*

Opposite: *We slept in the vehicle some distance away so we could get into the den before first light and be there for the morning play time.*

Right: *Feeling the growth within her,*
*Legadema tested everything in her world with needle-sharp teeth.*

Opposite: *The cub was a ball of energy from the beginning.*

# FOOTPRINTS

While tracking with the Shangaans and the San since I was quite young, I marveled at how after hours, even days, on the track of one animal, something would suddenly click, some transcendence to another realm, where the tracker could not only see where the track was, but, they say, could see through the eyes of the animal they were tracking, that they could feel the heartbeat of that animal overlaid in their chests like a twin being. They could foresee what decisions that animal would make before it made them and in essence they became that animal. It's about accepting that wild heart into your own.

Before man lost many of his instincts, he moved according to these same rhythms. Beverly and I try to live by this same ethic today. It's not easy. We aren't San or even born in the wild, and I have to say that if we have to step back and travel away from the bush, it takes a long time to sharpen that internal edge again. But somehow tracking has become as big an obsession for me as filming and telling the story of big cats.

Two days after we first found her, Tortillis decided to move from her den because some hyenas came nosing around. We saw her go, but we were new to her world, so at sunset we left her so as not to impose too much or expose her too suddenly to our presence…plus we were bone tired! We were also concerned that our presence may attract the hyenas.

The next day we searched around for Tortillis and knew that tracking her and her cub was going to be harder than expected. Unlike tracking lions, which is a little like walking on bulldozer tracks through a desert, following a leopard is a very delicate process. Here, the dense forest woodland of Mombo had sucked her up and closed in behind.

We drove back to where we had left her and I said to Beverly that I would simply track her the long, hard, old-fashioned way. I said "simply" but my mind was saying: "There is nothing simple about tracking a leopard!" I couldn't even find a single track despite knowing exactly where she had walked the night before. Her footprints had dissolved into the dust, almost as if she had backtracked and smoothed the sand behind her.

I've looked down at lion tracks for at least 28 years, but as I picked up the first faint impressions of a leopard footprint in the sand that day, I knew that this was going to be a whole new learning curve, and a change of mindset.

*In the beginning Tortillis moved the cub every three days and chose a fresh den.*

Old Alphonse, my Shangaan friend and teacher, taught me to never make an assumption in life. He was applying that to tracks, but it is good advice for all aspects of life. Assumptions lead to mistakes. So he made me see each track in the sand before moving to the next. In my youthful arrogance I would want to jump ahead to the water hole and check that out, get a jump on time, speed up life…but it was one step at a time for him.

Lions walk straight for long stretches of time. Leopards float, stop, switch back, circle, do 180 degree turns for no apparent (visual) reason, and then the tracks disappear. Usually the reason for a switch back is not because of any other track on the ground, but because a monkey or squirrel has spotted them. I looked around to where the next track should be, except the ground was completely bare of any marks. I walked around and around, careful not to mess up any ground ahead of her, but still impatient to get going. Finally, after another hour, I went back to the first and only track and took a breath. As I looked at it up close, I could see the depressions from the four toes in a slender pattern. She had a sharp track, and this was her back foot, so much sharper still. I stood up, away from the mark, and in the mid-morning light, it nearly disappeared.

I examined the footprint again and a tiny piece of sand rolled into a depression, as if it was eroding in front of my eyes. It was like a boulder for me and I could hear it creak with effort and crash down into the depression of her footprint, because the other thing about tracking is that besides what you are seeing (or looking for) in the sand, you are aware of movement around you. In any case, you are always closer to the ground than you think, and every other sense is on high alert. Time slows, if you let it, and you can almost see the patterns in between the light waves beating down on you.

Suddenly, as if I was watching one of those trick holographic images, it all popped into place. I could not only see the track I was staring at all along, but the next one and the next. I could see a flick of sand to the side and I knew that she had lifted her cub into her mouth and been thrown a little, just a little off balance. It was such a shock to me that I blinked and jerked back as if I had been slapped. I stepped forward and followed for 10 or 20 paces at normal walking speed. I had her direction but in this I was taking no chances. I would not leapfrog ahead.

But then that moment of complete and utter creative bliss ended as I lost the track. This time, instead of walking back and forth, angling the sun to see highlights, looking for broken grass stalks, I stopped dead. This time I had nothing in my mind. I waited and looked at the last track and slowly scanned forward of the tip of the toe marks. If I saw nothing I would start again, combing the ground, stroking it back and forth with my eyes, and then settling on the one track I had.

Without moving a muscle for 15 minutes, I became so relaxed that I could have fallen asleep were it not for the fact that my mind kept sharpening by the second, and the forest was yelling in mega decibels all around me. Then it popped up again, a line of tracks, 10 or 20 of them across the bush, the last one still new with a slight flick of sand…she was still carrying the cub. It was as if I could see her doing it, as if I was watching a ghostly replay of the incident.

Tortillis had stopped, adjusted the cub and set it down, leapt into a low tree, and had looked around. Her cub had tried to follow and had fallen off the tree trunk and waited. Maybe that was what prompted her to come down and lift it again. She stepped over it awkwardly, two back feet tracks on one spot as she adjusted and flicked the sand before she walked off again. I knew without a doubt where she was going up ahead. I could see the low cover, and my mind walked with her, imagining her, breathing with the effort of carrying a cub. The lines between us blurred…I wanted to make it to the trees in case I was spotted by a hyena or lion, or even a jackal. I felt vulnerable moving fast, low to the ground. I was her.

I didn't move directly to the trees but instead tracked each footprint one by one for the next nine hours. We spoke little in that time, as Beverly drove the vehicle behind me, observing the forest and keeping a listening watch, understanding that this was as much about finding the leopard as it was about the process for me, a way to understand.

While I tracked, Beverly listened to the forest for any other signs or clues to where Tortillis might be. A sudden flurry of birds, baboon calls, monkeys, squirrels, small cisticolas. Her ears are like a hawk's eyes!

As I walked and stopped on the track, I was aware of the decisions Tortillis had made maybe an hour or two ahead of me. I was making them too. Step onto an open patch and avoid snapping a twig that may attract attention. After a while, it was obvious what she would do, what choices she'd make. The long grass covered her but it also brushed against her whiskers, making her fold them back, shutting down an important sense for her. The grass flicked noisily against her ears and she had to turn them backward too, leaving her even more vulnerable to what was ahead. So, eventually she, and I, avoided the long grass.

In the next patch, she turned left and skirted along the edge of the grass. I smiled. I knew why she had done that. She stepped into a slightly muddy patch and shook her paw in irritation, and again I smiled and caught myself flicking my hand, my mock front paw. Now I was reading the tracks more easily but not with my eyes. I moved slower and slower. Instinctively, I knew we were close; the consistency of the sand grains that depressed under her weight had not yet loosened up. I looked up at the tree line. She was in there somewhere. I caught a vision of her in a low tree like an X-ray view behind the forest and then Beverly suddenly switched off the vehicle.

A vervet monkey called a single squawk.

"Up there. They've seen her," Beverly said softly, triangulating along the line of the monkey's stare, but careful not to stab me with volume in her voice. We track leopards a lot and some days are like this—still, a zen-like ride into a gravity-free floating experience where the science of knowing the biology of the animal and the physics of the weight and footprint, agree to partner with something else in your head. Maybe it's the heat. But to shout or bump or interrupt with anything but a "find," or real danger, is like waking a sleepwalker.

And in a moment, we found her lying up in a low branch, just as I had visualized. When we arrived, she didn't even look up. Why should she, we'd been walking together for nine hours.

# TOUCH

Each day in the field is a journey, sometimes a war of wits to find a cat that has evolved to stay hidden. It requires engaging the science of knowledge, logic, and thought, as well as that inner meditation to rise to the leopard's level of understanding. Legadema's mother kept making it harder and harder for us to reach this level.

Once we did find the cub, we sat nearby and watched, slowly morphing into her world. When her mother came back from the hunt, it was as if that spell was broken. She led two lives, one with us and another with her mother, the two never overlapping, until one day.

She was a few months old. We had been sitting nearby for three days, just Beverly, our vehicle, Legadema, and me…and the irritating squirrels above. We moved every few hours as the sun slid overhead and tried to outsmart us and beat us with its stinging rays, chastising us for our inertia and stupidity of being out in the midday heat, day after day. The cub played and slept, hissed at squirrels that she knew she could not get to, and slunk away into the shade or long grass when baboons wandered by. She was invisible.

Then in the distance—we heard it the instant she did—there was a cough. Tortillis was coming back. Legadema's legs moved faster than her head and she bumped against the overhanging Croton tree. Cough. On the third, more urgent call, the cub was off like lightning, leaping like a fox on the hunt, and ducking under trees and long February grass. Her mother was coming for her.

It caught us off guard. Cameras, lenses, tapes, pens…it was a rush to pack and move. But the grass covered a dozen acacias broken by elephants over the years and any sort of haste would have been stupid and noisy. So we sat there and decided to listen to the reunion. But Legadema stopped. A moving mound of grass gave her away, but she had stopped. Then, we heard the first call she had ever made, a seven-month-old's version of a cough, and as we watched, she turned and tunneled her way back to us and poked her head out. We weren't following, and she was waiting! She looked at us and called again, more loudly, like you would if you weren't being listened to, and waited.

I started the engine, and she relaxed and turned again in the direction of her mother. At that moment we knew that we had somehow embedded ourselves into her world, as she had in ours.

*Together but independent, this almost aloof independence is so characteristic of leopards, even from an early age.*

Above: *Mother and daughter spent the next year nearly attached, bonding carefully and constantly.*
Opposite: *Like a replica, Legadema copied every nuance of her mother, even her walk.*

By the seventh month, as Legadema moved more with her mother, finding either or both of them became a massive task. Each day we were waking earlier and tracking longer. But looking back at our journals, I see that 84 percent of our days we eventually found them. Getting something on film was another matter.

But maybe we tried too hard, like when I forced myself on the tracks I so desperately hoped would reveal their secrets. Standing silently, trying to unravel tracks in the bush, is a silent meditation.

*I stand silently*
*Staring, waiting, hoping, yes,*
*Foolishly perhaps.*
*Looking down at sand.*

*Sometimes you make me wait hours.*
*And then at last, breath.*
*You come to me, a vision.*

*Small, mysterious.*
*Temptress that you are, I know.*
*You have left me signs*
*And I smile, yes, I know you.*
*Yes, your foot was here,*
*And there and again over here.*

*Your tracks betray you,*
*But they don't lie about you.*
*Nor do they just say*
*Where you have been today.*

*The high-level play sometimes went wrong as the less-confident Legadema slipped and fell, saved only by a bite to the neck from her mother. Hauling the cub up delicately saved it from falling 20 meters to the ground.*

What makes a good mother? Someone who cares, who nurtures, who protects. If there are Ying and Yang in the world, leopard mothers must provide both, and of course that is possible. That supple feline agility and gentle nurturing, set against the switch to physical huntress—dashing through the undergrowth to sink her claws into a flank to anchor it just long enough to slice hard and fast into the cranial apex with her two-inch-long teeth— is such an interesting contrast.

It is the same as the switch from perfect relaxation to intense action that always fascinates me about the big cats, and leopards display that more than most. It is what has made our job so interesting and so hard. One minute the leopard we are watching goes from a three-hour slumber to a mild stretch to disappearing in an instant, only to come up out of the grass with blood on her whiskers. (This is usually followed by curses from the camera vehicle.) But it is these moments in your life when you know immediately that some kind of everlasting magic has just happened. A look you will recall forever. A moment in time that few people will witness and you may never see again.

We look at each other, both with similar thoughts, and say, "Are we lucky? Is this going to be an easy shoot? Can we even voice such things?" The answers are, "Yes, no, and yes, you can voice such things but beware…" Many a researcher and filmmaker have made the mistake before and thought that they would get many chances at these kinds of moments. They take it for granted and anticipate that if this is what one finds on day one, imagine what an accumulation of three years of days will amass! We've learned to never take it for granted, shoot it now, and well, and leave a future day free for something else if need be…and never voice anything that may foolishly tempt the gods to sneer.

*You are part of me*
*I know. I feel that warm glow.*
*That gentle hunger.*

*When apart from me,*
*You linger in all my soul,*
*A memory you,*
*A near ghostly companion.*

*When close by you touch,*
*Just the mere glance of a touch.*
*And it is enough.*

*When photographing a leopard, there never seems to be an awkward pose. Each curve is shaped as if*
*in harmony with every backdrop. It's why they can mold into everything and disappear so easily.*

We all have wild eyes, or that passion for wildness within us. But from this, creativity is sometimes born and nurtured, and in Legadema we could see this creative thought process. Her wild eye would turn to a sudden softness and she would race around, trying to understand the world surrounding her. That process of observation is so much a blend of what she was when she was born, some bundle of hard-wired cat instincts that had her stalking through the forest looking up at squirrels or birds without ever having seen her mother kill an animal. We know. We were there the whole time and through any phase that she could have seen a kill. And yet she knew how and what to do. When she saw a young impala off in the distance, she became a killer.

We watched as Tortillis twitched a moment too early. The baby impala would have walked right over her, but instead it stopped and stepped away. The moment was over. But Legadema took the opportunity and dove for the impala, morphing into a streak of fur and unsheathed claws. Her solid teeth used for crunching bone pinned the struggling animal without applying enough force to kill it. This baby impala became a sacrifice to the development of the young leopard.

Legadema's delight was obvious. But what was stunning was that she knew exactly what to do, where to attack, how to hold the throat, when to kick with her back legs.

What she did not have, however, was the training of what this was all about. She had never tasted meat before! The mauling went on for hours. Finally after some serious hair loss the impala was exhausted and Legadema was getting frustrated with her friend. Her mother looked on with as much interest as she might have watched a hornbill pecking at a hole for termites. Once, as the impala made to escape, Tortillis stepped in, grabbed the throat, immobilized the antelope, and returned it to Legadema, alive.

But then it was as if some magical light bulb went on. The cub, now only a few months old, watched and then dashed in and tumbled over the impala with a perfectly executed throat hold kill. The conclusion we drew was that very little in her final makeup could be qualified as purely innate, inherited from nature, or truly learned from her mother. She is a cocktail of influences…as are we.

*For months she had seen her mother return with kills, but when the first live fawn was brought in, the real lesson began.*

*Still very much a cub, Legadema attacked and played with the baby impala but didn't have any idea of how to kill it.*

*She was too young to understand the difference between "play" and what she had inherited from her mother's instincts.*

Above: *We'd read about suffocation being a technique used by some big cats, but at last we had clear evidence of that.*

Opposite: *Twilight—when dreams can turn to nightmares for cats as hyenas stalk the ground.*

# A Step into Our World

One day we were positioned against a sloping tree and she walked over, smelled the tree, and jumped up. The curve of the trunk took her up and over us until she settled down to rest no more than three meters away and almost above us. We could see every hair on her face, each fleck in her eyes, and while it was almost uncomfortably close, she had chosen that distance and we decided to stay. It was 7:00 a.m. She went off to sleep and after some dramatic close-up filming, we also settled down quietly. But Legadema, like most cats, seldom sleeps as we do, 100 percent unaware of the world around us. Her ears work the sounds of the forest even when her eyes are closed. Her eyes open the narrowest of slits every few minutes to check on the world around her. On this day, each time she opened her eyes, she looked at us. But it was a different look. She looked at Beverly and watched every movement she made.

As Beverly dusted the front of her camera, Legadema cocked her head at the motion, and then when it was over, I could see her look into Beverly's face as if to analyze what she would do next. It was midday and the three of us had been engaged this way for hours almost at touching distance. Beverly quietly suggested lunch. "Should we move off?"

I looked at the situation and wondered if starting up the engine right under her would give her a fright. "No. Let's stay."

Beverly slid into the back of the truck quietly, but nonetheless Legadema watched each placement of a hand or foot as she went over the seat. As Beverly vacated her seat, the cub's eyes widened. I looked over to see what Beverly had done. Nothing. It was the fact that Beverly had opened up a space and suddenly Legadema slipped down the tree and took the two paces it needed to get to where Beverly usually sits and with an effortless jump, she was in the front seat! She sat there like a tame Labrador, or as if she was used to the position, and looked at me from inches away. She sniffed the gear shift, the pens, and camera pieces I was using, and ran her nose along the small rail that Beverly uses to hang onto the dashboard. It was a shock for us!

I reached over to the heater switch. A hot blast of air must be like what comes from her mother's mouth at these moments. Our heater, as a result of no doors and no roof, collects all kinds of debris and had a leaf caught in it; it would rattle as it blew hot air. As she looked up at my hand moving to the control, her ear came close to the vent and the heater blew at her, slowly at first. No reaction! I moved it to the next level. The leaf rattled. Legadema opened her mouth in a silent hiss to match. At Level 3, and with a look of reluctance, she stood up and left the car, giving a rare cub call as she left. It broke our hearts, but it was necessary.

Completely by accident, we became a part of this picture and this story, despite our strictly drawn rules and boundaries for the project. I think one builds barriers when seeing kill after kill, filming as much of that as possible, and engulfing yourself in the hardship. We have recorded thousands of kills, both of lions and leopards, of lions killing each other, and leopards killing lions…death, death, death. Over the years, we had developed defenses against becoming too attached and involved. But at the same time, we also developed a great working method of not becoming too detached and allowing an understanding of our subject in. It was a balance and part of this attitude of ours was to keep us on track. We were doing well. Then Legadema stepped into the truck!

Over the next few months, she tried over and over to claim that seat. I decided to use the exact same message to her each time, and in some strange reverse taming, we managed to get her to understand that this was a boundary we needed her to obey.

*In between more important hunts, she usually found time for another squirrel or two.*

# SQUIRRELS

From her tenth day on Earth, Legadema had shown a keen interest in squirrels. It was remarkable. She could barely move around the forest floor before the squirrels called their alarm at her from high up in the ebony trees and she could recognize the irritation on the air.

We watched her look up and scan the trees and lock onto the sound. We noted in our journals that even at less than two weeks, leopard cubs are capable of hearing and pinpointing a sound in the treetops with accuracy. In fact, she found the source before we did.

Then she charged around, looking for the nearest access to the squirrel. Running while looking up is not easy, even if your legs are only two inches long. She ran into a twig, fell over and took a roll, backed up to continue the run, fell off balance and hit the floor again, before leaping up once more onto a log, and at last to the base of the squirrel tree, all without losing visual contact with the offensive squirrel.

At five months, she had tripled in size. Her legs had some strength, her focus was honed to a degree where we noted that as she stalked a fat squirrel squawking at her, she flicked her eyes down to the base of the tree once or twice. We wrote that at this age she had cognitive skills that included preplanning. She was thinking into the future, planning the split-second route she would take as she would race over the thicket, under the log, up to the tree, leap up and latch onto the broken limb that would take her weight but not that of a larger cat. She had this road map in her head as her front foot twitched off some sand, her tail jerked—a foreshadowing of what her back muscles were going to do a moment later—and she was off.

We followed with our cameras, under the log, over the thicket, onto the tree and the exact limb, because I had watched her eyes making those decisions in that silent inactive moment before the action. She dived and swung around, dropped out of the tree, and literally bounced back, grasping with claws and dedication at the slippery squirrel. She did not kill that fat mother that day. But she logged up one more experience, and we could see her slowly arming herself, as clearly as if she was a young Wakumba warrior winding hand-beaten arrowheads into stiff reed shafts and assembling the arrows for another day.

It didn't take long. Her first successful squirrel hunt came as a bit of a surprise, to us and to her. By six months she was like a cat with ADD. A squirrel in the forest would launch her into fits of quivering, tail flicking, and paw shaking. Then she would race, bounding up to the tree top, and down, a frenzy of action for hours each day. Sometimes her failure would leave her clearly disgruntled, coming back to the shade of the car growling and letting out a low, miserable groan with raised whiskers and a wrinkled nose. We would hear her slip in under us and rest up against a wheel, and then moan whenever a squirrel called up above. It was just a rest period. This was obsession.

On this particular day she was hot. It had been her tenth exhausting tree-top-and-down rally. Some of the leaps were more leaps of faith than calculated hunting moves. One had left her tumbling through branches for at least 10 meters. How she reached out and caught herself before smashing to the ground is a small miracle of balance and agility that is "leopard." So at midday, she retired to the base of a Leadwood tree, panting, sore, and grumbling. She looked at Beverly as if she wanted her advice…or the softness of her seat.

Just above her a squirrel started up. Legadema moaned and flicked the offender a look that could have killed if it had any energy left at all. She didn't even roll onto her shoulder, her favorite resting position. She lay flat out in the sticky burs and thorns too tired to even move when the sun found her through the thin branches. The squirrel chirped and leapt around in a display probably not designed to actually taunt the leopard, but it was clearly having that effect anyway. Legadema was beat and not at all happy.

But she did muster enough enthusiasm to look up and stare once more at the leaping squirrel. It was a male, and he leapt closer onto a low branch. I filmed and framed to capture this disgruntled look on the cub's face, while keeping watch on the squirrel with my other eye. For many people this split dual view of the world with one eye through the lens at one scale, while scouting around with the other is a dizzying experience, but it is the best way to prepare for the unknown.

Suddenly, though, something happened that we had never seen before or after. The squirrel lost its footing and came flying down from the branch at the surprised leopard. As the squirrel struggled to recover, a nicely kept set of young teeth closed around its neck, and Legadema had her first squirrel kill. It was a moment that perhaps tipped her playful relationship with squirrels, (certainly that particular one!) and took her to the next level. During our time with her we saw her kill more than 200 squirrels!

When we saw her recently, as an adult of five years stalking a young zebra, a squirrel spotted her and screeched. She looked up, and I couldn't help myself from saying "Oh oh!" In an instant she had plotted her course and scurried her way up, over the fork in a tree to a springboard of a branch and off across to the squirrel. The next I saw of her was as a bundle in the grass with a glint in her eye and a furry ball in her mouth. It was, and maybe still is, an obsession with her, if that is possible in a "mere animal!"

# WILD EYES

Yes, I see your wild eye. This is a phrase I silently tell myself almost every day I see her, almost like one of those irritating mantras, or words from a song once enjoyed, now stuck on rewind in your head.

But this one is almost a private moment, when she looks over at us with that look that is anything but wild.

These animals have characters, and we cannot ever expect to find another like this, in the same way that I could never find another as perfect a match or companion in personality as Beverly may be for me. There is something about the way she moves, something in her eye that entices me—Legadema, that is! Both maybe. But it is just so arrogant of us to assume that we are the only species in the world that is a collection of individuals of different personalities and characteristics beyond the physical.

We find timid leopards, mysterious ones, loners, bold ones, playful ones, and Legadema, a cat with something of her own within those eyes.

When she spots a movement in the grass, something ignites, some deep interest, and I want to say mischief, but some would say that this is attaching too much unknown and human emotion. And they would be right. But at that moment, what is going on? The tortoise races for cover at a blistering few inches a minute, but the cub must know she cannot eat this. She plays, rolls it over, pounces and lies on it, taps at it, and then uses it as a cushion to sleep on. So what is going on? Experimentation, most definitely, but to what end? If we cast everything that animals do into behavioral categories, we may sometimes miss out on the things they do just for fun, just like us.

And in those soft, interested eyes, I also see that wild eye, and I love what I see, because I hope, in the deepest hope of all hopes, that I have it too.

*Hey there, hey now you,*
*Did I catch that look in your eye,*
*I see your wild eye,*
*Laughing! Is it really there?*

*That softness and shine.*
*Side by side with blood.*
*They will say that is not right.*
*"One or the other."*

*In you, they walk together.*

# THE HUNTED

Legadema was just learning how to move around at night alone. It was hair-raising for us; many a cub has been lost at night.

One day we sat with her through the day and watched as she slept for a full 12 hours. Not the most invigorating day of our lives, but it happens, and you never know when it will happen. At dusk she came down and started to move around. She was still very young, just out of the nursery school of learning how to interact with even the smallest impala. However, there is no confidence like the confidence of youth, and she ventured out. We looked at each other and, possibly as a result of the uneventful day or this exploration, we tagged along at a distance.

A scream from the scarlet sky raked across our nerves. Baboons came racing past us, and a huge male baboon erupted from the grass nearby with a wriggling baby impala in his mouth. He sank his vile-looking teeth into its spine and looked around. Baboons here seldom move around at night, so even a male his size is clearly vulnerable. Legadema was out in the darkness somewhere, and we imagined her to be lying low, terrified.

Suddenly the male baboon jerked up and leapt out of the tree, abandoning his kill. We looked around and saw our small spotted cat running in. The night perspective may have been confusing for the baboon, and he may have misjudged her size. She was no more than three months old, maybe twice the size of the average house cat. Normally his reaction would have been exactly the opposite. Baboons have been the one consistent threat to her life.

This night, Legadema ran in, sniffed around, and located the dying impala in the tree and tried to scramble up—just as two hyenas arrived, alerted by the desperate death calls of the young antelope. Everyone arrived at the tree at roughly the same time, and while Beverly tensed up, thinking that Legadema might appreciate a warning of some kind, she was bound by our code not to interfere.

At the last minute Legadema looked over her shoulder into the gaping mouth of the first hyena and bolted up the tree next to us, hissing and spitting her displeasure. The hyenas stole a part of the kill, but Legadema plonked herself on top of the rest of the meat and waited them out. At dawn she was still in charge, surrounded by thorns just out of reach and as the hyenas wandered off, Legadema picked at the meat a little and lost interest as well. She scrambled down the tree and walked off, returning to the large ebony where she had spent the day before just in time to hear the francolins calling nearby. Her mother was back for her. As the two greeted we got a sense that Tortillis looked up at us, trying to piece together information to give her clues to why, when she left her cub with us nearby she was clean and in pristine condition, and now she was full of thorns, smelling of impala and hyena breath, and a little shaken. What could we say?

*The full moon almost gives us back our slight visual advantage, a handicap we share with baboons.*

A cub, a teenage cub especially, is such a bundle of energy that its mother can be worn out quite easily. At first we thought that Tortillis was being unbelievably diligent in going off hunting for three or four days at a time and leaving the cub (with us!) despite her motherly instincts to be with her cub.

One day she came in to check on Legadema. The two greeted, then played, and within an hour Tortillis was having her tail attacked and her ears pulled. She got up and stretched, skipped to a higher branch and across to a far tree and off again. We decided to follow. All she did was move off beyond cub-following-range and settled down again for the day.

The whole of that day and the next she simply lay within range but nowhere near the cub, only returning to suckle once and to lick the burs out of the cub's fur, then back to another distant tree to survey the forest and rest up away from the torment. But even in this we imagined that link as an invisible thread between them, strung out taut across the trees, a listening watch being maintained all day but in a collective awareness rather than any one sense.

Sometimes the mother's link to her cub is so aware that other things in the forest can creep up on her.

Legadema was off doing things that we have never seen another cat do. She was smelling flowers and playing with butterflies! Pink flowers (cats tail) and brightly-colored butterflies. Each flutter took her another step into the forest, and while we could still see her, we got a sense that Legadema was wandering off into trouble.

The dark shadows were looming, but not behind the cub. Tortillis was watching the cub go off track and turned to follow. Then we saw the shadow. A male lion was stalking in behind her, no more than a few paces away, slowly stepping in through the grass. He looked down and took another step and even though we were some way off we could hear the twig snap. Tortillis took a moment or two to register the sound, then as she turned she came face-to-face with the huge hairy vision of the male lion. She swirled and sprung up, bounding away for safety, for any retreat or bolt hole, and found a tree easy enough to fly up in a few leaps.

The heavyset lion bumbled along after her but he was no match for her speed. Hers was a race for life; his was a game. But it showed the difference in bulk and speed between these two big cats. It also showed that despite their complete focus, a leopard can be caught out in the forest, where there are always surprises, especially at Mombo, which has possibly the highest predator density in the world. Our statistics from our observations show that this place is richer in lions and leopards than any other location we have studied in Africa.

*Distracted and looking for her cub, Legadema's mother very nearly walked into the jaws of death.*

*Blood drips from your jaws,*
*Cold ice dances in your dark eyes.*
*You are a killer,*
*A thief of hearts, a player.*

*Oh all I know here,*
*You understand every move.*
*You are Africa.*
*You are my dark inner heart.*

*Sometimes, it can all go wrong. In Mombo, leopards can usually retreat to*
*the safety of the trees, but if they get caught out in the open, it is over.*

From the earliest age, Legadema was aware of the threat of lions. She heard them each night. They visited her second den and moved on without seeing her. Over the years we've seen lions leap up and tear leopards out of trees, but in the open area between palm islands in the Okavango, there is no place to hide, and lions often surround them and attack. Eradication is the ultimate goal. It is thought that predators kill each other most often to reduce competition for food, but who knows what a lion sees when a lone leopard walks out of the trees nearby.

Legadema grew up as a single cub in an area with her mother, occasional visits from her father, and perhaps one to two forays from the neighboring leopardess. In that same territory she was likely to come across around 22 lions!

But due to development and man's encroachment on the lion's territories, the lion population has now dipped under 20,000. Because lions live in prides, they are unable to withstand man's expanding footprint, while leopards, solitary and elusive, can adapt more easily to man's presence.

For me this is the best indication of the future. As we pick away at the edges of preserved areas with our hunting, poaching, cattle farming, crops, and finally, cities and roads, there is a shockwave of intolerance of big cats that increases and leaves only the most independent to survive like fugitives in a forest of development.

There are other threats to leopards in the wild, sometimes more sinister and less immediate than the lions that will hunt them down.

While the night belongs to the leopard, the day is owned by dozens of others. Baboons and other animals that harass them during the day are not safe under the cover of darkness. We filmed and photographed very few scenes with these leopards at night. It was a conscious decision. Leopards are not isolated animals despite their solitude. They are so much a part of the forest. We often call them ghosts, as they seem to vaporize into the undergrowth. It was that ingredient of them that we wanted to get across more than anything else, so in many ways our challenge was to find ways to avoid showing the leopard front and center in frame. I wanted to film images where the cat appeared as if magically and disappeared as fast, and it is during the day when this happens even more. At night they move around much more openly, less afraid of detection. So we decided to show them during the day so we could better place them in their habitat. Lights and strobes tend to highlight the subject and that was exactly the opposite of what we wanted to do here.

But even at night, leopards don't have it easy. Although we weren't trying to capture images, we spent many a night with Legadema and Tortillis and were very aware of the long trail of alarm calls from baboons, jackals, birds, and virtually everything they walked past. It is testament to how difficult it is for them to move around unseen.

The moment every now and then, when they drop that cloak and give in to reality, is the instant of the kill. As they attack, they have to dive into our world of reality, and the forest of watchers explodes with fury, alarm, and conspiracy to reveal the spotted ghost.

When they kill, they have just seconds to cover their tracks and get that kill spirited away and out of sight, because lethal as they are, they aren't the largest predator around, and are not very confident on the ground. Hyenas are always waiting for the forest to erupt, and know what the chirping squirrel calls and vervet monkey barks are saying.

At least half of Tortillis's kills were lost to hyenas.

*Their ability to chase down and catch more than 30 different species at Mombo is one of their most enduring strengths.*

# GROWING UP

In time, of course, Legadema grew up. She started going with her mother on territorial patrols and nudging her way innocently and eagerly into adulthood. Ironically, as she matured, she moved more into our lives and started interacting with us more, but it was this mother and daughter relationship that consumed us and them. This was the time that was probably the most exciting for both cats. They often moved through the forest as a duet, catching things off guard, Legadema learning to hunt, to patrol, and to be a leopard, Tortillis in a rare moment where she had a hunting companion.

If she was mostly hard wired before, this was the next phase of her education—when what she learned from her mother added another layer to what she was, and what she would become.

They visited Tortillis's favorite trees, a range of about 20 giant trees or ones with cool and comfortable limbs. Years later we still find Legadema in those same trees looking out dreamily as her mother did while the cub pulled her tail. It makes me wonder if there is any memory of her past in these eyes. Does she see a tree and remember that it is a well-known refuge from her days as a cub? Can she reconstruct a memory of the first time she saw the tree and leapt up into its giant canopy ahead of her mother, driven perhaps by the scent of her mother's previous visit? Does she remember her mother? We define ourselves in part by memory, sometimes hanging on to who we are in perspective of those memories, sometimes allowing ourselves to grow and create by not having too perfect a memory. I wonder where leopards lie on that scale.

It has been said that only humans have the ability to remember the past, be self-aware in the present, and think about the future. After years of testing this one theory for validity over and over with many animals, I have to suggest that an animal like Legadema is well aware of the past, extremely self-aware of the present, and can contemplate the future.

For example, we had been away for some months after our filming, and while editing the next film we arrived back in Mombo and found her sitting on a termite mound. Nearby two safari vehicles parked quietly, but as we arrived, I heard one guide say to his guests: "Watch this! Look at the way she is looking at them. They've been away." And within a few minutes, during which her eyes never left us, she stood up and walked over, passed the two vehicles and went straight to Beverly. She looked up into Beverly's eyes for a long minute or two, and then blinked, slid under the vehicle and up on my side. She looked up at me as well, almost as if shaking loose the cobwebs of time in those memory banks. She sniffed at my foot and gently held it in her mouth like a bird-retrieving dog might for an instant, then she walked straight back, not looking at the other humans, and settled back down on the mound again.

Even now, she often looks at her own reflection in water and in our lenses, cocking her head back and forth, and she does many things that indicate a forward-thinking ability, like plotting the foot positioning to go up a tree in a glance, or planning out a strategy to circle around and ambush some prey moving to water. She knows where the water is, knows the low ground to get there, and anticipates the forward play. Her time with her mother may have taught her that. Our time with her has shown us that so much more is going on.

*For us, sunset represents peace, tranquility, the end of the day and its heat. For leopards, their day has just begun.*

Above: *Ambush practice—developing form and style of hunts through play.*

Opposite: *And yet each attack was gentle and playful, neither exposing claws or biting hard.*

# ACT II: THE TURNING POINT

She made a mistake. Her mother had killed a decent-sized impala male and had hauled it up into a tree to get away from the hyenas. It took effort. Tortillis has a bad back. It shows in her eyes, small dark spots in the iris confirming what the scars on her back show and the logbooks at Mombo Camp speak of. Baboons had attacked her when she was young and very nearly killed her.

But her kill was safe and it was time to collect her cub. Legadema ran ahead like an excited cub, despite being 13 months old already. She could smell the effort of the kill on her mother and she looked up at each tree ahead in anticipation. If a leopard can smell the tracks of another leopard three days later, after a mild rain, the scents of this must have been like tiny explosions of senses in her head. When a droplet of blood touched her shoulder, she snapped her head up and took five leaps from trunk to branch to canopy before the patch of red on the sand could soak in.

Tortillis was tired and lay down as the cub mangled the impala. Like many individuals of that age Legadema decided that the carefully selected perch in the fork of a tree that her experienced mother had chosen was not quite good enough. She grabbed the impala, nearly twice her weight, and moved it to her selected position, unfortunately one without any fork in which to wedge it. The curved horns snagged in the previous fork and suddenly Legadema found herself hanging on to the carcass as it went over the edge. It nearly pulled her off the branch but she dug in her claws and held on to the dangling impala. Tortillis leapt up, and in three bounds reached the kill just as it slipped and landed on the ground.

The thud was meaty, wet, and solid, enough to jerk the heads of three sleeping hyenas nearby into high alert. They knew exactly what it was, and faster than Beverly could pull off three images, the first hyena was in, the two leopards that had jumped down to rescue their meal were out, and the meat had changed ownership.

*Her goal is to hide and stay hidden. Scavengers arriving for the dropped bones and blood will mark the end of her feeding time, so she covers every tiny scrap from them.*

Above: *Tortillis's message was clear in a very visual way, those teeth exposed to their fullest and most vicious.*

Opposite: *The end of a mother-daughter bond, that instant of defined independence comes as a shock, a sadness, but a necessary stage of development.*

Tortillis was spitting mad, growling and hissing, not just at the hyenas (but at us too! I don't know what we had done!), but mostly it was Legadema who took the heat. She tried to recover the meal for her mother but the huge hyenas chased her off over and over again. At the height of the dance, a troop of baboons arrived and Tortillis moved to cover. As Legadema followed, the foam of rage lined her mother's hissing fangs and bubbled with her fury. If there is ever confusion about a leopard's deepest inner feelings, this face set those aside. Every visual aspect sent the same signal as the sounds of anger, and it was a turning point in their relationship.

But as Tortillis hissed and struck out at Legadema, the cub did something quite amazing. She regressed into submitting in a way much smaller cubs do, as she did when she was much younger. She called very light cub calls, something she had not done for months, but all of that was expected. Then after circling and rolling submissively, without any reprieve from her mother, she turned to us and came right up against the side of the vehicle where Beverly sat and looked up at her and called over and over again, before coming to my side with a similar appeal.

Perhaps she saw us as a dominant force in her life in a similar way as the dominant force of her mother, and in trying to submit and appease one, she needed to appease the other, too. She rolled over on her back and patted out in our direction, calling over and over, submitting, appealing, hanging on to some vestige of her old life.

From that day on, Legadema was no longer her mother's cub. She was expelled, and we never again saw mother and daughter tolerate each other anywhere in their territory.

She took to wandering alone. What choice did she have, this expelled little female not yet a huntress, no longer a cub? Her world was empty of companionship too early.

*She looked at us as if appealing for something, some intervention…she was a cub again.*

# CURIOSITY

One day, in an attempt to get at least something of her on film, I slipped out of the vehicle and moved away. She was asleep underneath, and after a while she got up, stretched, and came over to see what I was up to. I turned the camera to her and perhaps because of the changed angle, the flat lens front reflected her image back at her—another leopard! She came up curiously though now she was well used to seeing us, but this reflection really got her going. She purred a low noise and put her nose up against the lens in greeting, then when only cold, hard glass greeted her back she patted at the face in the lens playfully, rubbing it with her paw. Then she circled behind me, but without any view of the new cat there, she quickly came back to the lens. She soon tired of all this and went back to the vehicle to rest, leaving me out in the sun.

When we flew out to get some editing done, we parked our vehicle at Mombo camp. A week or so later we got a message that we needed to come back and either move the vehicle or do something about the leopard that was sleeping under it all the time because the staff couldn't get any work done! She had tracked us down even though we weren't there!

If baboons came by, she'd slip to safety under the back wheel. Hyenas passing saw a head pop out and retreat again, and once she hid from vervet monkeys that were in the trees above for six hours until they lost her and stopped their chattering. Eventually they swung off to more exciting mischief and left us alone.

Gradually she crept off and buried herself in her own hiding places for days, making it nearly impossible for us. Finding a leopard not much bigger than a decent briefcase in 20 square kilometers is tough enough, but once we did find her, it was an exercise in tenacity to keep her in view. Either Beverly or I had our eyes on her all the time, possibly 18 hours a day. If we looked away for a moment and she moved, we'd never know if she had rolled over in the thicket or walked out the back, and be lost to us for weeks. We'd do hand offs…saying, "I'm going to get some water, over to you…" and on and on through the day.

She was alone one day, and investigating a sudden movement in the grass. Still squirrel-obsessed she jumped in over the tall grass—onto a snake! It whipped around at her and she arched herself out of the way and escaped. But as we watched, she lay down again and started to lick her back leg.

We looked at each other. Had there been a strike? An hour later as she tried to move, we knew that she had been bitten. She was salivating from her mouth and her head drooped down. Clearly she was in pain, and she kept the back right leg off the ground, even when she lay down again, to keep her two legs from touching. I've felt the coal-hot sting running through my veins from a neurotoxic snake bite and I understood what she was feeling. Every membrane, every cell, is on fire and your head rages with throbbing pain.

This small leopard did what her instincts told her to do. She went into a thicket and slept it off for three days. We felt her pain.

We have always wanted to find out more about the nomadic phase of the lives of big cats, and we had this opportunity at last. Most times we see cubs grow up and disappear. Many times sub-adult males arrive from some other place and we don't know their past. Following Legadema was the first time we could gather this information.

There is a connection between the forest and the huntress that exists as a collective balance that never stays quite the same. When a leopard makes a kill, the balance is thrown one way for a moment as the energy flows back down into her muscles. She drops a piece of meat, and despite her best efforts to avoid the pestering hyenas or vultures, they will eventually catch her out and take some for themselves. Slowly the life flows back through the system, never lost but in an endless river, never quite the same but always flowing, always returning in one form or another. It is only us that are able to flick the switch and stop that flow, or let it drain out onto the floor without regard, meaninglessly.

More and more, we seem to lose touch with that inner exploration. The less we trust nature, the more we see it as something that opposes us.

*Up high she is safer, with a greater vantage to view her piece of Africa.*

*You are alone now,*
*Cast adrift on a wild sea.*
*Grey shapes growl at night,*
*Fangs, tusks, stabbing eyes.*

*You are alone now,*
*Too young to know your way.*
*Too old to go back.*

*Your only soft companions,*
*Floating in your veins,*
*Are millions of years older,*
*Your guides, your instincts,*

*The ones you lie with at night.*

*She has a precise idea of each hole, every tree, and her next den within her range.*

# A NEW DIRECTION

We drove out of camp one day and Beverly suggested we go west instead of the way I was headed. The day before, we had left Legadema far to the south and I was just a little anxious to get back to where we'd left her at dusk. A lot of things can happen overnight but it is seldom a major change in location. My feeling was that the best place to start the search was at "ground zero" from yesterday. But we've both learned to trust a hunch! It was a beautiful morning filled with life and the sounds of buffalo and zebra calls. So we turned west and I searched the road ahead for tracks.

Then, Beverly heard something in the forest.

"Yes, elephants," I said, not without some irritation. It was getting late in the morning, and already the light was looking great.

"She's with them."

I looked at Beverly standing up on her seat looking into the forest.

"Yeah?"

She nodded. I took a deep breath and counted to 10 then turned in and slowly maneuvered the vehicle through the broken trees, gingerly driving through thick grass, feeling for holes with the wheels, ducking under low branches in the forest until we worked our way into a clearing with the elephants. The peach-colored light cut through the forest, painting the elephants beautifully in their arena.

I could feel Beverly smile because there was no word or movement from her to cue me otherwise, and when I looked over, she was looking up above the elephants, at the softly draped shape of Legadema, exhausted from a long walk, safe up high from the elephants but with that same smug glint in her eyes that Beverly now had.

What Legadema was doing, of course, was working her range from one end to the other, educating herself, developing a road map of features in her head. When elephants catch her out in the open, she jumps up a tree, or runs to a hollow log—places she has bolted to before or checked out at leisure. Slowly, a young nomadic leopard becomes less nomadic, less of a stranger here and more secure.

She was laying down her anchor.

*Despite the size difference, the least dangerous animal for leopards is an elephant.*

*I know your sharp eye.*
*I have walked through this valley*
*Many times before.*
*The water is full of dragons,*
*A huge ball of fire.*

*It will smile on you,*
*It will dance on your white bones.*
*Beware, we may watch*
*Your journey to nowhereland,*
*But you walk alone.*

*Beauty in death.*

She survived on a diet of squirrels and loneliness. We watched, sometimes for days without talking ourselves, silent witnesses to the void in her life, not thinking about the void she may leave in ours if the squirrels ran out. The forest didn't let up on her. It had its upper hand, and as this immature female wandered around she made one mistake after another, stalking up to zebras only to be caught out and chased hell for leather through the undergrowth. Too many times she ended up in the thick thorns of a low acacia hebeclada tree where not even a baboon could reach in and drag her out.

Beverly's consumption of the herbal tincture called Rescue Remedy increased with each narrow escape Legadema pulled off. It's a tonic that calms the nerves after a shock. Beverly started carrying some with her all the time! But Legadema survived, more often by pure fluke than by design. The Grim Reaper was just not paying enough attention.

Slowly, like watching a dead body revive, we saw her start to gain strength. She was getting her old inquisitiveness back. That old mischief started to glint in her eyes again. She stalked in on mongoose and impala, zebras, and even elephants, most of which chased her off course but it was a start. When the elephant bull she was tracking with serious intent turned and spotted her at his feet, she fled directly back to us and ducked in under the vehicle, only poking her head out again after we had been charged, covered in dust, and then looked underneath at her. She took these two peering faces from either side as an all-clear signal to at least uncover her eyes again.

It was during this phase that she made our vehicle, and us, a constant in her life. As a regular platform for shade, it was a place to get some peaceful, hidden sleep where—unlike the trees—the shadow of the vehicle never completely worked its way out from covering her. The odd drip of oil didn't seem to bother her. At first we thought her use of us was quite wonderful. As we spent hours parked out in the baking sun while she enjoyed the shade, we started to wonder who was using whom exactly. At first we sat quietly, not wanting to disturb the resting cub. Later we learned to just carry on as normal—she didn't care one way or another! We bumped around and made lunch, cleaned cameras, and basically went about our business with one exception…we couldn't film a thing; our subject was under the car!

At one stage we happened to be on a track when some baboons came by. Once again, Legadema slid in under the vehicle and hid, then moments later went to sleep. We were parked there when a Mombo Camp safari vehicle drove up and parked next to us aiming the opposite way. The guide greeted us politely and asked if we had seen anything unusual around. As I hesitated and looked down, I could see the tip of Legadema's tail slide to the side, away from the other vehicle's wheel. As a precaution, she pulled her tail in so it wouldn't be driven over. All I could muster was a tight-lipped shake of the head. I didn't want to put the guide in the position of having to explain to his visitors why there was a wild leopard under our car!

Later I told him about this, and all the guides then made a habit of reading the mood in their vehicle, and either looking under our car or driving off. Mostly, though, Legadema became known locally as having developed a special bond with us, and we spent many enjoyable hours sharing her closeness with a handful of safari-goers who visited Mombo from around the world. Today, people visit Mombo specifically to see Legadema, which is wonderful of course, but I feel a need to apologize to the guides for adding this pressure to their lives. She doesn't always want to be found.

*Who knows if she ever really believed that she could catch a zebra, or if it was just something to do on an otherwise dull day.*

# Baboons

From an early age, 12 days exactly, baboons were part of the fabric of her life. They weren't a positive influence. On that day, they raided her den and tried desperately to drag her out by her tail. Legadema's mother was also in the fortress of fallen down tree branches, hiding like a cub herself. The view from inside the hideaway—with huge male baboons barking, their open mouths filled with broken teeth—must have been terrifying. Terror indeed is exactly what baboons use against leopards here, and at every opportunity they attack or chase a leopard into hiding. Legadema's mother carried the scars forever. Even her father made sure he disappeared at the first calls of a troop nearby. But she and her mother shared a territory almost exactly the same size as that of a major baboon troop and one has to believe that they knew one another intimately.

Even on a kill, a time when one would expect to see more of a defense, both Tortillis and Legadema, and just about every leopard we know, will drop down out of sight at the first distant calls of the baboons. We hadn't seen this before, and many scientists and observers from other areas had seen different reactions. In some areas, baboons are often prey to leopards, and run scared at the sight of them. At Mombo, the baboons run directly at anything that resembles a leopard.

The level of aggression ranges from a mobbing attack, where the cat is isolated in a thicket and surrounded while the larger males reach in to grab a tail or chunk of fur, to one case where a young male leopard was caught out in the open, flipped over, ripped, and bitten in the stomach. Had he not managed to get to cover, I have no doubt the troop would have killed him.

News travels fast, and these kinds of incidents don't go unnoticed. Legadema stayed up a tree one day when the same young male leopard was harassed once again. She knew exactly what might happen someday if she got caught in the open.

The only serious retaliation we ever saw was when Legadema was four months old. An elephant was shaking a palm tree and Legadema slunk off to take a look while Tortillis dozed in a thicket nearby. As the cub moved, she drew the attention of a troop of baboons that had silently moved in behind the elephant to steal some of the rewards of his palm-shaking efforts. The baboons burst into attack and we saw four huge males charge, leaping over fallen trees to get to her. She bolted, but as the males passed the thicket hot on her heels, Tortillis exploded from cover and went for the leader, with a flared mouth and flaming eyes, spitting and kicking up dust. The baboon got such a fright that the attack was called off and they all disappeared in a matter of seconds, but Tortillis and Legadema took half an hour to find each other and console one another.

Baboons are not to be meddled with if you are a leopard.

*Mombo, and Botswana in general, is going through a phase of massive baboon increase. Troops are reaching 120 strong.*

Above: *After she had killed the baboon mother, she probably didn't expect to find a days old baby baboon clinging to its mother's chest.*

Opposite: *At 13 months she pulled off the impossible, a baboon kill.*

She was alone one day, testing the forest, and suddenly she dropped down into the grass evoking her magical powers of invisibility. A moment later, we watched the baboon leaders and scouts come through, their darting eyes looking for one thing only: spots in the grass.

The troop walked within paces of her. Then a straggling female baboon swayed through the bush, and to our absolute amazement Legadema poked her head out and dashed forward, stopped, and trotted in again. It was like a suicide attempt. Any noise and the entire troop of more than 60 baboons would be all around her in an instant. But she was swift and silent, and before the female baboon could utter a gasp, her throat was clamped shut and she was struggling for air. The blood flow to her brain was cut off a minute later and she relaxed her grip on the leopard's fur. Legadema had made a major turnaround in her relationship with these lifelong rivals and Beverly and I looked at each other and smiled. It was a first for her, and a turning point in her life.

As she hauled the kill into the low limbs of a fallen tree, something moved in the baboon's fur. A newborn baby baboon, no more than a day old, struggled to change his grip on his dead mother's hair. As he did so, he tumbled off and fell into the grass. Legadema took a moment and looked down at the little baboon as if she could not quite figure it out.

We positioned to film the sad event of yet another baby animal getting chomped in half, but when Legadema jumped down, she sniffed and looked at the baby and then lay down next to it. This needed some thinking out. When a lone hyena came nosing along, she quickly lifted the baby to a safe place in the tree and hissed at the hyena from nearby, a warning that she never gives when defending her food. She was warning the hyena off, away from the baby!

For the next four and a half hours, she lifted the baby whenever it ventured off to a dangerous place in the tree and replaced it gently and safely. Once it fell off and she jumped down alarmed and lifted it up and put it back on the branch, as one would a wounded bird. It got colder and colder. It was July and our winter was setting in; the desert sands that overlay the Okavango hold none of the warmth and turn cold suddenly. The baby baboon felt the warmth, and reached out for it, and then cuddled into a surprised Legadema. She hesitated and then turned her warm neck to the infant and the two rested together for hours.

I don't know what was going on inside her head. But having come to know her well enough, we understood that this was different from the cat-and-mouse style of playing with squirrels. This wasn't a cub being curious anymore, and she wasn't being predatory right then either. She was too young to be a nurturing mother, but perhaps it was all of these things bundled up into one, or all three fighting at the crossroads within her. In some way, the baboon may have signaled something of his own to Legadema. If he had run away, I am sure it would have been a shorter story to tell! His appealing posture and reaching hands bought him a little time.

*What we didn't anticipate was the quite amazing response to this baby baboon. Instead of killing it, she nurtured it, saving it from a hyena at one point and grooming it.*
*The baby baboon responded likewise, following the leopard and finally nestling into its neck for warmth and comfort.*

She didn't eat the baby baboon. The cold night, shock, and the lack of nutrition all took their toll and the tiny, almost inaudible calls went quiet and stopped. Legadema then sniffed the infant, patted it once or twice, then stepped away, looked back, and jumped up high to where the mother lay grotesquely wedged in a knob thorn tree with a leathery and disturbingly human-looking hand, frozen in position like that of a beggar's last appeal for mercy.

No kill has ever been quite as interesting to me as that baboon. The conflicts within Legadema seem appropriate perhaps to our sensitivities. Killing executed without remorse of thought seems inhumane at least, and to see an animal hesitating is intriguing. To think about someone who may save up to fly over here, desperate to feel the sensation of pulling a trigger or worse, releasing a carbon fiber arrow into the heart of an animal for the sheer thrill of it, without remorse, is disappointing. I often look into the eyes of animals, animals that trust us as she has trusted us, and look away out of guilt and embarrassment.

I remember trekking up into the volcanoes of Rwanda and eventually finding the gorillas we were seeking. We took our pictures, filmed some beautiful scenes, and then something happened. The silverback looked up from feeding on some wild celery and looked into our eyes. Nearby I heard Beverly whisper after a moment, "I'm sorry."

It was a private apology from us all. We can do better. If killing gives us joy, we are doing something badly wrong.

Legadema, by contrast, must live by her own code, one that inclines her to kill for a living, and it would be ridiculous to draw a parallel between what she does and what a safari hunter does.

*She seemed to be trapped at the junction where cub instincts of play meet leopard instincts of hunting, but with an added element of maternal instinct as well.*
*And finally this conflicted cub went off into the night with the baby baboon in her care. For the next four hours, they lay down together.*

*The lions we work with seem to have developed a habit of licking their lips moments before starting a hunt. Legadema is less predictable, but sometimes she will lick her lips when she hears impala in the distance.*

*I see your wild eyes*
*Turn soft with our reflection,*
*A certain knowing.*

*Thank you silently,*
*Privately perhaps, and go.*
*You have things to do.*

When the little pigs emerge, the whole atmosphere changes. Gone are the dark days of dusty winter and straw-colored grass refuges for leopards. Gone too were the tense days of Legadema's dependence on squirrels. The green grass erodes some of her camouflage skills, but as these lightning-fast little warthogs dart for safety in confusing directions, the leopards have to use other skills altogether. It's a fast racing, twisting and diving, tumbling chase that mostly ends in a cloud of dust as they duck down into their holes in the ground, safely leaving the cat casting around in confusion.

Chasing warthogs has an added risk: the parents' tusks even make me shudder sometimes as I track along, head down, and surprise a warthog. We've both had one too many cornered against a thicket as we came along and had to side-step smartly as they barreled past, gnashing their teeth and grunting in disgust. Tortillis and Legadema have been treed by seriously angry pigs who flick spit at them from below.

So when struggling little Legadema reached 19 months and the rains released the next class of piglets into Mombo, we wondered if the lessons had been well learned. The best of these lessons was that Tortillis seldom hunted pigs in the field. She watched them and waited for them to return home, then if the parents were out foraging, she risked the venture into a hole. It's a difficult position to be caught in; tail up while your head is snatching for trapped piglets, but when Legadema was almost five months old, she watched her mother do exactly that and in an hour she herself harvested three sucklings.

As we followed our young leopard now, she tested the mother pig. We sighed—would she ever learn? But from the thorn tree retreat, she could see where the piglets went and the game was on. And it was a waiting game. As she circled the den we could hear the grunts below. So as to make sure we weren't interfering, we backed off some distance and added long lenses. It took an hour, but at last someone's nerve broke. Three little warthogs made a dash for it, and Legadema, despite a face full of sand, launched a running attack. Following circles within circles and ever widening patterns in the grass, we traced the route the pigs took to escape. All escaped but one!

To fully understand this you must imagine that release of energy, that elation of success after so many failures, that sense of relief of being given a lift up after being so close to becoming another leopard without a name, just another failed cub of Tortillis the mother. And you will forgive the explosion of joy that followed as she thrashed around in the grass, replaying the hunt over and over, leaping at the dead piglet and tossing it up in the air, catching it and bouncing up and down trees and away again to hide and do it all over again. It was the day of one dead pig, but many, many kills!

That day her distinct whisker spot had blood on it and she was enflamed with her success.

*Pigs in holes are a difficult and dangerous prospect for anyone who approaches.*

*Warthogs are as stubborn as they look.*

*Legadema's youthful chases caused chaos in the warthog family.*

**Following spread:** *Hunting, running, and chasing down little warthogs as they dart for cover is clearly worth the effort, as seen by Legadema's father, Burnt Ebony.*

*The result of a reckless hunt, this young piglet was the most succulent of all the treats for leopards here. Suddenly Legadema exploded with playful leaps and mock attacks that, at the risk of sounding anthropomorphic, seemed like pure joy.*

*We both knew that look.*
*It was the wild look and more,*
*Something beyond that stare.*

*She was transformed now,*
*Alive, vital and ready.*
*She was a huntress.*

*A thousand generations old.*

*Slowly Legadema developed the thicker neck and upper body strength she was lacking as a baby.*

# LEARNED OR TAUGHT?

When Legadema was a three-month-old cub, she was left alone while her mother went off hunting. In the convoluted way of many hunts, Tortillis was led back near where her cub sat waiting and watching from the undergrowth. From this point of view, Legadema was able to witness something incredible.

Tortillis hunted the monkeys up and down trees for hours, unaware that she was being watched. The small, intelligent apes had her fooled at each move. It was a three-dimensional chess game high up in the trees. But finally, the leopardess was beaten. It showed in her shoulders. She turned with dignity that barely showed a crack, and walked away. Legadema stayed hidden.

Then suddenly, Tortillis switched back and flashed up into the trees, flying higher and higher with each leap until she was above the monkeys and looking down at them. There was panic. Monkeys like to command the high ground. Now all it would take is to fake them out and force them to make mistakes. Legadema was sitting nearby and her eyes darted with the huge, dilated pupils of a jade dealer seeing the biggest gem of his life.

When one monkey decided to freefall from 40 meters and take his chances, Tortillis threw caution too. They landed seconds apart, and how she didn't break every bone in her body I have no idea…perhaps it was the small grey cushion she landed on!

Legadema had learned a valuable lesson, and in our film *Eye of the Leopard* we used this moment as inspiration for many moments like it. We could see the same ideas being triggered within her as were triggered within her mother, and we recognized exactly the same hunt played out from years before.

We watched her make her first major kill as a teenager, her first against the vervet monkeys. As she dragged the fur off her prey, her eyes darted frantically, manically, filled with adrenaline. Amber tension. Balled up shoulders and loose limbs stretching, reaching for the tree that would transport her to safety. But I looked closely for the arrogant self-satisfaction, the gloat, the glee of success, but it wasn't there, although in a strange way I felt it stir within me. In Legadema, I saw life—acceptance of now, and that's all, no expectation, no glory, no passing of age, just life, today, tomorrow, and as it should always be.

*Legadema chose a different tactic this day. She watched, then darted across and got higher than the monkeys, and then hunted them down. Usually, it's the monkeys that get to the tops of the trees first.*

*Above: Only very rarely do leopards actually manage to catch and kill a monkey, although the hunts can take hours.*

Opposite: *Legadema's half-brother has an undaunted sense of adventure, even taking on honey-badgers despite their ferocity. The bite he got on his nose was not nearly as bad as the stink of the spray of urine he got in the face.*

# THE ELEGANCE OF MATURITY

Gradually we found that we were following a mature leopard. She was a survivor but still skirting around her mother whenever she heard the rasping adult call in the distance. I think they both knew what was going on.

Legadema was biding her time, living each day one at a time, from squirrel to warthog as we followed on behind.

Tortillis was giving her some space, but often made surprise visits to the area that Legadema frequented. On those days, Legadema disappeared! We would search for days from corner to corner of her range and find nothing. We'd go farther afield into neighboring lands of hostile females. Once we found her wandering four territories away from her birthplace searching for some space away from her mother. We followed her, constantly walking, without more than 10 minutes rest every few hours, for two days.

We lost her one night so far south we worried about having enough fuel to get back to our camp 30 kilometers away. When we woke at dawn, there were leopard tracks around our car. I measured them. It was Legadema.

Searching, searching daily. She for a place to live, we for her or any sign of where she might end up.

One day after a rainstorm had washed all tracks clean, she suddenly looked up right into the face of another leopard. Legadema attacked!

It was a dark-looking female, somewhat bigger than herself, but as she turned back with lashing fangs and exposed claws, we all recognized the other leopard. It was Tortillis, the wet but indignant owner of this territory! Legadema hadn't recognized Tortillis because all the rain had obscured her scent so much. Legadema was severely beaten and raced up into the tallest branches where the heavier leopard could not balance and sat there until it was all clear. Then she picked her way out of the thorns and came to lie down next to Beverly.

Around this time it was inevitable that she would start to be courted by some male.

Seeking a mate can be a problem for leopards. The only male Legadema ever came across was her father. She was aware of her half-brother, the cub of another female and her father, but as she was reaching maturity and becoming a beautiful young leopardess, we knew that she must be attracting attention.

But the leopard conundrum is that the time difference between birth and successful ascent to adulthood is just three years, and most males will still be in charge of their territory by the time their daughters mature. The fail safe is a built-in avoidance of males for a while. Even then the first few batches of cubs seldom make it, and later, as the female reaches five, it is unlikely that her father will still be around.

We caught a new male in our headlights as we drove back to camp one night. We doubled back to see if he would interact. He came in cautiously. She saw him coming, and stood up to watch. He sniffed the tree and looked at her kill. She circled but instead of going to him, she came to us and stood behind the vehicle uttering a range of rude-sounding calls—coughs and snorts and growls—but she was reluctant to leave the safety of our presence. He didn't seem to take much notice. Then, as he coiled to spring up and help himself to her meal, she stiffened her legs and strutted forward, growling gutturally, careful not to venture too far from Beverly.

He took one look at this and uncoiled, dropped his tail and slipped off into the darkness. Beverly looked at me and said, "Hmm, maybe this is the one! Maybe he'll be her mate." And without a hesitation, I answered, "What? That scruffy looking youngster? Never."

*From early on, Burnt Ebony's solitary nature made him a very good hunter.*

# BURNT EBONY

Legadema's father, Burnt Ebony, had the cold calculation of probably the most precise hunter I have seen in the cat world. And yet he weighs not much more than an average man, certainly smaller than a rugby player. In those eyes, though, you sense that he would destroy any man or beast he would want to, in a stroke. He is in complete control as he views a warthog or lifts his nose up and trails the scent of a newly born animal—which is exactly what we watched him do one day.

The buffalo had moved through, leaving a swath of flattened green grass and the rich (not foul smelling) aroma of fresh dung. They had run into trouble with lions, churned up the earth, swirled through the forest, stopped in the open, and then disappeared the way they had come. The tracks told their story.

When we found Burnt Ebony, he was in a tree keeping well off the troubled battlefield. He slowly got up and sniffed the air. Some say that these big cats have 20 times the sense of smell that we do. In the case of leopards, especially this leopard on this day, he picked up the smell for something a half a kilometer away. He was down the tree in a flash with a nearly silent thud. He glanced nonchalantly over his shoulder at a patch of beige in the grass—another cat, much bigger but by contrast much duller in its spot-deprived skin. Then, some young male lions woke and bobbed their heads like oversized domestic cats and stalked in pretending to hide. The leopard stopped and looked at the lions' pathetic attempt at stalking in unseen and unheard. He blinked them away as he moved on two or three paces and disappeared in the grass like Houdini.

When a leopard disappears, we are all tempted to look closely at that spot. But the trick, of course, is that exactly where you last saw it is the worst place to search. Like that famous magician, who makes you look at one hand while the other is conjuring up a rabbit, cats leave you with only a swaying stalk of grass to look at while they slip away. We circled and found him much farther away than imagined, and as we looked back we smiled at the trick that left the two lions smelling at the exact point we had lost him. What he was homing in on was not a half-decayed carcass but something fresh. Adding another layer, he stopped and swiveled his ears, small ears not built for precision, but still better than ours. This time we heard it too.

In the dense undergrowth a baby buffalo had been born and remained in hiding, alone, silent except for that one call. It was immobile, relying on a half hour's worth of experience and millions of years of instinct to stay quite still. The only thing that he could not control was his smell, the slightest milky smell of veal!

Burnt Ebony's nose had pinpoint accuracy, and an instant before he stopped, we saw what he was searching for. Our cameras moved quickly and the small black head of a baby calf poked out at the sound behind him…and then there was the snap of a twig under the soft paw in the undergrowth.

Opposite: *Splayed wide like a net of claws, nothing can escape.*
Following spread: *Burnt Ebony is the only leopard we have ever known that has caught a buffalo, in this case, a lost calf.*

*The kill is a dance,*
*A struggle to eat or live,*
*Who takes away life?*

*Some god, some magical man*
*In a hat, priest, Death?*
*Or the slice of claw,*
*Bite the neck, shake the soft flesh,*
*Hold the throat and clamp,*

*That glorious flow of life,*
*To my mind, to yours.*

*Any other leopard would stay safely up in the tree, but Burnt Ebony had a natural disdain for hyenas and descended to express his displeasure.*
*The visual code that is universally known as a threat comes through exposed weaponry, in his case, sharp teeth and a knowledge that he would use them.*

# THE END OF THE CYCLE

There are purple days. And there are days when you want to breathe in and soak in the beauty, because just finding a leopard draped across a huge limb in a tree is gift enough, but when the light comes out and spotlights her against the season's darkest sky, I often hear Beverly utter something next to me.

"What?"

"Nothing."

But it is something, it is everything actually, an involuntary expression of when everything is right: the day, the light, the success of finding the leopard, life. It is a gentle thank you, and the satisfaction of knowing that when that shutter springs an image into being, and we hear the echo of it closing, we know we have not only saved a moment, but perhaps by framing it one way or another, actually made it into something.

In the beginning of our careers, Beverly would ask after some moment if I had captured it. Now there is no need to ask. Not that I manage to film everything beautifully, but there's no point in asking. These gentle grunts and expressions tell it all. We could live with the close relationship we have had with wildlife on so many levels and never film or photograph a thing, but the addition of adding a layer of art to that is very satisfying. But is it enough?

Working at this time of the day with the palette of the best that an African dawn can give you unites all the best things in life in that instant. It is not just a scratching of the surface, it is a moment for reflection as well. As hard as we work, we always set aside a part of the day, at dusk or at dawn, to watch the sunlight and to silently celebrate where we are, where we came from, and what tomorrow might bring. Then inevitably it ends abruptly when one of us says, "Boy, the mosquitoes are fierce, aren't they?"

*Dark, brooding skies paint a perfect canvas to highlight a cat in a tree. Dark days are good days for us.*

We had to leave. Our filming was over and needed to be edited. We had to turn in our film to National Geographic Channel, and the international press was lining up.

Legadema was ready. The cycle was complete. The rains were dumping so much moisture on us that we got tired of putting the vehicle cover on and taking it off, so we sat in the rain more often than not, knowing that it would dry later. But at some stage it didn't dry out. Any leather belt or shoe started a colorful growth of green mold, and following Legadema was a mess of getting stuck, winching forward, or digging out of the mud for hours.

We knew we were delaying. We flew in one day after a visit to the north and landed late, hurried, and not as softly as one would hope. I wasn't piloting this day—a friend Paul was flying us in as a favor—and on landing I noticed that he was getting quite busy in the cockpit. Beads of sweat formed on his forehead and we seemed to be going quite a bit faster than I would have liked. I asked if he was okay and he said, "No brakes!" At that he went off in a loop and swung it around to a point where instead of giraffes, we had trees in front of us and we still seemed to be doing quite a lick.

Perhaps it would have worked out, if we didn't hit some ruts. They took us from a fair speed to dead stop, nose and propeller in the dirt, and tail in the air, in a cloud of dust. Beverly's camera came out of her hand and went between Paul and me like a canon ball and hit the dashboard and windshield. A wheel came pretty close to coming off (it dangled on a thread), and apart from a little blood from somewhere I never quite figured out, we all stepped out and dusted ourselves off.

The plane wasn't good, but we were fine. Two days later, Legadema walked to that spot and sniffed around briefly and went off to her favorite fig tree just to the north of the airfield. I wonder what she smelled.

*Africa is a place where leopards float through the treetops like silk.*

It hurt deeply each time we needed to fly out even for a day or two. I remember putting off a flight for days, one day at a time. Finally we packed our small Cessna at six in the morning and turned back to the fresh mist rising over the floodplains to breathe in the last pure breath, as if it would fortify us as we headed for town, only to hear a crackle on the radio.

"Yes, go ahead."
"Dereck, we have Legadema at the old sausage tree on Maun Road."
Beat, beat. I looked at Beverly. She thought hard, privately adjusting calendars in her head.
I looked back at the radio.
"Thanks, Francis. We'll be right there!"
To Beverly, "Tomorrow, we'll fly tomorrow."

We followed her through the wet season, and delayed flying out day after day and eventually we were two weeks late. We knew we were both waiting for some event, some turning point so we could step away with some comfort and satisfaction.

It was dusk, and the sky dimmed beyond orange and even further to scarlet and then a dull inky blue. I put the camera away but kept following. I knew what I was doing. I wasn't letting go. Finally Beverly reached over and touched my forearm. I stopped and turned off the engine, and Legadema carried on into the gloom. We picked up binoculars, stretching out the last light while I heard a giant clock tick loudly in my head.

Then, suddenly in light we could barely see through, the shape of her body stopped and turned. I could see the sharp movement in her shoulders and stomach before we heard it, but she looked at us and started calling, a deep rasping fully mature leopard call, one that would be heard everywhere in her territory and send the message to anything within that space.

It was the first time we had heard her make that call. We looked at each other and smiled. I politely let her finish. She looked at us as if we needed to follow. We wanted to, but we didn't.

And she slipped away.

We released our film and Legadema was seen by millions via our discussions on morning shows and on the film itself. We worry about the decline of all cats and have something to say about that. When India, the home of the tiger, has fewer than 1,200 left, you know the road to extinction is smooth and short. We could be in the same place in Africa before we know it.

So as filmmakers and photographers, we are now thrust into the limelight as ambassadors, in a way. When we escaped all the attention and flew back home to Botswana, it was as if the dark clouds of the city were leaving our lungs, and we both longed for some days alone with Legadema. But finding her was going to be a challenge.

Guides at Mombo were sending us mail saying that it had been months since a sighting. All leopards seemed to have taken a dive in numbers and some blamed the lions again. Legadema's mother, Tortillis, was missing. Her half-brother was long gone, and Burnt Ebony, as they called her father, was dead. It was chaos. We flew in and landed and wasted no time trying to find any sign of tracks. We visited all the old favorite trees and trails.

Although we found leopards, most were skittish and ran off and it privately felt like we were walking through the leopard equivalent of the Valley of Death. In the distance we saw some lions eating and went over, only to see them sniffing and eating the body of a leopard! Was it Legadema?

We checked with binoculars, no spot. We moved on, tracked, searched for weeks. I revisited my rusty tracking routine, which had really lapsed after five months away from leopard tracking. I woke one morning and said, "She's at the old sausage tree."

The Bushmen or San people manage to reach into their intuitive side more consistently than anyone in the world. Their methods are arguably the most primitive as well. There was a time when to survive or to do well, we too needed to tap into something higher or more in depth than our day-to-day lives, beyond that immediate drive to advance one step at a time.

We checked out the sausage tree only to find that the secret nocturnal contract she and I had made the night before was an illusion.

The decline in leopard numbers at Mombo was overstated; we tracked 19 in that time, a delight for the guides at Mombo, but as we left each one behind for them, our hearts were heavy. To help our research and observation over the years, we made detailed measurements of Legadema's footprints from impressions in the sand as she had grown up. Her back foot measured 7.14 cm when we last saw her, and I wasn't expecting a late growth spurt. This tactic came from a day when we were tracking Tortillis and the trail led into a thorn thicket. Instead of ripping my back on the thorn, I circled and smiled at the words from old Alphonse, the tracker, to never assume anything but to look at each track. I had jumped ahead anyway. We followed on for hours and finally saw her sitting in a huge tortillis tree. Tortillis in a tortillis tree made perfect sense, so I returned to the vehicle and drove in. It was hours before we figured out that this was the wrong leopard and Tortillis had most likely smelled another female who had marked that tree and headed off in another direction! Alphonse wasn't deserving of my smirk and I started collecting measurements using an engineering tool.

*Soft evening shadows may highlight her for a moment, and then as the dappled light passes over, she will disappear once again.*

Finally we found a cat in a low tree one day who looked small enough to be Legadema but darker. Beverly worked on getting some images, and as we were ready to move on, the leopard turned and Beverly froze. It was that spot between the two long rows of whiskers on the right lip. It had been five months and two weeks, and Legadema stood and stretched nonchalantly, like a mature female. She slipped down the tree and across the open area between us and straight under the vehicle! We were back, and she knew! Within minutes, she was on the move, and just as soon, she walked into baboons again, and they chased her to cover.

As we sat with her, she settled and we realized that we were doing exactly what we had done for four years with this leopard; we were carrying on as if we were filming, making a film, but it was all over. What we did know was that she was safe, well, she was more than safe actually. More than a survivor. As she went through the grass, we noticed a certain thickness around the hips! That scraggly young male!

We followed when she moved and at one point she stopped and we looked up at what had disturbed her. A hefty male baboon balanced on a dead tree just ahead. We froze, she was way too close and he was clearly the scout, a big male with perfect teeth that he yawned in our direction for show. If he looked down, he was sure to see her at the side of vehicle. I knew she would withdraw discreetly, but readied the camera anyway, for what, I did not know, since our filming was over.

But Legadema didn't withdraw. She launched herself at the male and charged, leaping up onto a fallen log the size of a small boat. The baboon yelped and flew off his perch and landed heavily on all fours, and the last I saw of him was his front feet coming up between his back legs.

She turned and lay down on the log, as if it was reclaimed land in a battle of wits. She licked the moisture from her fur and with a wet paw, cleaned off her still-long whiskers in the same way that a Persian cat does. She caught her own tail and groomed that as well, and suddenly Beverly and I looked at each other as if the same idea struck us both at once. It had. I pointed at the hollow log and she smiled and nodded. It was the perfect den!

*Legadema moves in and out of the forest with such ease and grace that catching a glimpse of her in the open is the exception rather than the rule.*

*It is a lifelong struggle, this one with baboons.*
*For Legadema, her rare successes may be cold comfort.*
*Virtually every day there will be some baboon disturbance in her life.*

# MOTHERHOOD

Legadema had two cubs on the 18th of January 2008. We saw them the next day. A few days later she came out of the den and led the cubs to the side of the car and stepped back. Why she did that, I have no idea. The cubs sniffed up at us with half-closed grey eyes and bobbing heads and tried to find their mother again. Just then it started to rain and she grabbed up one cub and ran to cover. The other tried to follow, so she dropped the first and picked up the second, but as she did, the first walked back to her, so she dropped number two and picked up the first and dropped it into the den and found the second in time to meet the first on its way back out. She turned and looked at us for an instant.

It was chaos and the sort of thing a new mother with two cubs has to cope with.

She looked as though she might cope quite well actually.

*When they were only days old, Legadema brought the cubs out and placed them near our vehicle one at a time and then backed away to rest.*
*We couldn't tell whether it was an appeal to help take care of them, some kind of introduction, or just a way to distract them so she could rest.*

*Previous Spread: The next generation of Legadema's bloodline, this cub's characteristics are inherited from Tortillis, Nicky (Tortillis's mother), and back in time at Mombo.*

*Right: It will be a challenge for Legadema to bring up two cubs, since she was never taught how to do that.*

*Some years are good years, others not. One year, I had to change 69 wheels.*

One day we followed her into a valley and slid down into the mud, wedged the wheels against a log and locked the car in an impossible jam from which I knew it would take us hours to extract ourselves. She was on patrol and we both knew we would lose her, and at this stage, losing her for an instant was losing her for days, sometimes weeks. Tension runs high when this happens, and each mistake costs us dearly, not only in time. I've broken bones, my nose once, accumulated deep cuts and weary muscles while digging vehicles out, and had a chance to be very creative with some cursing, so each time you take a deep breath and kick off your shoes.

Legadema swayed her hips off into the thicket and we knew we had to let her go for the day.

We winched and dug, and both got covered in enough mud that if anyone had come by they may not have known which of us was which. Then Beverly looked up and saw that we were indeed being watched. Legadema had stopped just down the path and came straight back to us. She stopped, looked at us, and the array of winches and jacks and tools, then jumped up into a low tree not 10 paces away and settled her head onto her paws to watch us.

Another hour went by and we were finally free, and as we smacked the mud off our legs and started up the engine, she stretched as well and carried on down the path where she had left off.

# ACT III

Our lives continue with Legadema, with some breaks to edit and follow up with our conservation work, but I have never felt quite at home as I do at Mombo and in Duba across the river, and never as peaceful as while sitting with Legadema, even when she is doing nothing. There is a certain knowing, a comfort among the three of us, heightened with the exchange of looks and these little interactions between a wild animal and us, bridging that gap that so few people have the opportunity to experience. I think the heartwarming moments are as a result of this almost unnatural companionship, but most are a feeling of mending something that we have so successfully undone in our divorce from the natural world. It feels like we are somehow healing that wound between us and them, one cat at a time, a couple of people at a time. It's not about taming the animal, it's about exploring that commonality between us.

Her one distinct spot between that long first row and the second is still, as always, a flag for us. None of her spots changed of course, none of the 840 she has. I know, there is something sad about a filmmaker sitting in the dust and heat in utter boredom counting spots over and over, but I can confirm 840 give or take a few.

But our ambition is to take this through the whole cycle, from birth to its ultimate conclusion, as sad as that will be, because no one has had that opportunity before.

She has also given us a deeper understanding and drive to do more in being a voice for big cats around the world.

*After a recent trip away, our return was greeted with a certain disdain.*

*As we watched and came to know Legadema and Tortillis, both of us realized how much we learned about them each day. For the details, Beverly uses a 600 mm lens and it is necessary.*

*The spot, in the whisker pattern, between the first and second row, clearly seen in these images, has never changed position.*

*Throughout her life, while other spots on her body may have shifted slightly, this one has remained in place, a guide for us and anyone who needs to identify her.*

With National Geographic, we started up an emergency fund for cats, The Big Cat Initiative, raising funds to bring attention to the problems that need to be solved right now, and to fund further action to save big cats as issues erupt.

In Maasailand, where there are now less than 160 lions, we are working with scientists and managers to get the Maasai involved in saving lions and leopards rather than spearing the last ones, and to do that we have to pay compensation for any cattle losses due to predators. Without creating an equal "balance sheet" with warriors and herdsmen we will never even be able to engage with them in dialogue about lions and leopards.

In Botswana we are starting similar projects. At the present rate, I doubt that lions will last 15 years. Leopards may sneak under the radar a while longer.

And when people ask what they can do, we never quite know what to answer. Of course, right now they can support The Big Cat Initiative with National Geographic if they are in a position to. But people should note that, in fact, we do not have to deny ourselves pleasures, as many people believe we have to, to save the planet. In truth, looking after yourself doesn't have to be as selfish and destructive as it first implies. Knowing that, you can investigate more, read more, feel more, understand all these things more, and slowly that loop closes back on itself and we understand that taking care of yourself means taking care of everything else. Conservation is such a negative word, like looking after the last species as the Titanic Earth goes down. But it doesn't have to be that way, and it doesn't have to be a hardship.

The one regret in even starting a project like this is that we know we will find out something important, some insight that may make leopards better to understand…and easier to kill. For that, I deeply apologize.

When the Greek leader Xenophon created enemies out of everyone or everything that was not of his army in order to survive, he left us with an attitude that manifests itself in basically hating everything that is not just like us. This extends to a type of animal xenophobia where we fear everything and believe that nature is out to get us. It's media hype, and you never read a newspaper headline that says, "Man kills leopard!" But if a big cat scratches one of us, it is headline news. That is probably because in the time we have worked with Legadema, 12,000 leopards have been quite legally hunted for trophies to hang on walls—not to protect livestock, or families, but simply for the fun of it. While we shake our heads and look down at our shoes, we are all partially to blame.

And so ends the journey into the world and mind of a leopard, for us, for now. We feel as though we actually achieved more than we knew we wanted out of this. Of course we gained more than she did, but perhaps we (she and us) can play a role in giving something back to her kind now. If it is only in helping people look at leopards in a slightly different way, in celebrating their intense vitality and knowing that without the chance of catching a glimpse of flashing amber looking back at us from the grass, we will be infinitely worse off, then that will be enough of a first step.

*Not a stranger to camps, Legadema wanders in and out of ours or Mombo Camp as if she owns them…which, I suppose, she and her kind do.*

# ACKNOWLEDGMENTS

To the people of Botswana who have accepted us as one of their own, the government, its Department of Wildlife, the Ministry of Wildlife, Environment and Tourism, and in particular its new President, His Excellency Ian Khama. You are all the shining lights of African governments, and an example for all leadership anywhere in the world. It's an association that we not only enjoy and thank you for, but one we are proud to be associated with. There is a new way dawning in Africa, under leadership that is true to itself and to the global community, and there has never been a more exciting time to be African, to be a Motswana. We thank you, the environment thanks you, and we hope that what you have begun in Botswana will be replicated in other regions in a wave of change.

To Wilderness Safari, who welcomes us into Mombo so warmly, as have the managers, staff, and guides there: Taps, Lizzy, Brookes, Francis, Celi, Alex, Malinga, Cisco, Silos, Brandon, Debs, Pete, Sharon, Simon, Jeremy, Craig, Simon, Buang, Thompson, and Tlamelo, in no particular order. Wilderness Safari executives, we thank you Keith Vincent, Grant Woodrow, Dave van Smeerdyk, Mike Meyers, Andy Payne, and Malcolm McCullough.

This project started thanks to Colin Bell, our partner in Great Plains, and to Keith, my brother who taught me, and continues to teach me to look at the world in a different, more exciting way where nothing is taken for granted.

To John Campbell, our trusted book agent, and to Charles Miers, Jim Muschett, and our editor Melissa Veronesi at Rizzoli in New York, Sarah Rachmann for helping with the layout, Robbie Frey and Dennis and Andreas at Silverton for great color work on the images, and to Lorna Gibson, who is our vital link to the rest of the world, and a compassionate Tortillis to Beverly and to me.

One last party needs a deep appreciation not only for years of support, for our films and books, but for our life's work, the National Geographic Society. They have become partners in a way that few realize and we are proud to represent the Society and what they stand for by being Explorers-in-Residence there. As we all try to steer our course through this time of confusing media, gushing misinformation in an over-hyped bombardment on our senses, it is a great relief to have the National Geographic Society as a mainstay. John Fahey, Tim Kelly, and Terry Garcia, John Griffin, and Chris Johns, we thank you. You all make us better.

Not surprisingly, we want to thank Legadema.

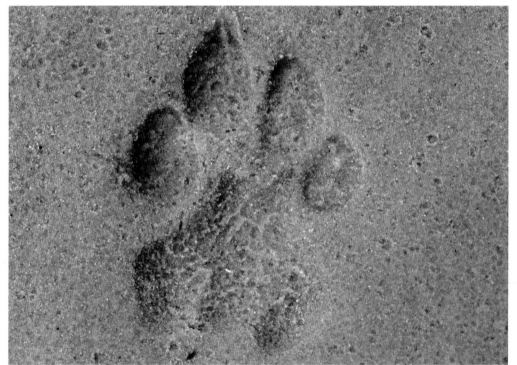

*Partial views of leopards are often the only clues, and most people will miss them. We miss them most of the time. But to stop and know that just up ahead there is a leopard is thrilling in itself.*